Make It Happen!

Make It Happen!

JAPANESE COMPANIES NEED TO ELEVATE MARKETING
AS A CORE FUNCTION TO SUCCEED OUTSIDE JAPAN

Robert E. Peterson

ISBN: 1511810084
ISBN 13: 9781511810081

Contents

- Marietta College, McDonough Leadership Center, Executive-in-Residence, *Communications Challenge* Program
- *Toyota Brand Forum* with Jim Stengel

Introduction
April 4, 2015

Japan is the world's third largest economy; it is an important country and will continue to be a valuable contributor to the global economy while the USA and China battle for the #1 spot.

In the 1950s, Japan competed largely on low prices, low wages and selling cheap imitations of western goods. Recognizing the limitations of this approach, Japan underwent a stunning transformation to compete not just on price, but on quality.

The practices and approaches Japan pioneered in doing so changed competition around the world, forever. Today, Japan must move beyond just quality and price to competing based on strategy and innovation. Genuine innovation not only in products, but also in approaches to competing will be required. One of these areas is the ability to influence, lead and persuade via marketing. As Japan has shown in earlier periods of transition, if mind-sets change, Japan has the capacity to move rapidly. A new national movement of no less significance than the *quality movement* is needed.

I arrived in Tokyo on February 25, 1982, for what I expected to be a two-year assignment; 33 years later I am still here.

I came to Japan because I am a marketing professional. The opportunity was created by a group of forward-thinking, maverick *Toyota Motor Sales* (now *Toyota Motor Corporation*) managers who realized Toyota needed outside marketing expertise to achieve their global growth ambitions.

I worked for one of the big Madison Avenue advertising agencies in New York City, *Dancer Fitzgerald Sample*, or DFS. DFS was appointed the ad agency for Toyota USA in 1975 and became Toyota's shadow marketing and brand management partner. DFS, through its Toyota advertising campaigns, defined the Toyota brand in the USA. This was the start of Toyota's journey to becoming the world's largest (by sales) and most valuable car company, as well as Japan's leading business.

The Japanese managers who appointed and worked with DFS in the USA were rotated back to Japan in 1981 to run the *Overseas Marketing Division*. Toyota did not have the marketing expertise inside the company nor among their Japanese agencies to effectively create and run marketing and advertising programs outside of Japan. Toyota needed western marketing expertise and approached DFS to establish a Tokyo representative office to work directly with them as internal consultants. Toyota wanted DFS to replicate what we had accomplished in the USA in other key markets. I was selected to be part of the initial wave of DFS guinea pigs to make this work, and it eventually did.

My new DFS Tokyo boss, Nelson "Skip" Riddle Jr., came to Tokyo first to launch the project and recruited me from the New York office to join him. He was 34, I was 29, a couple of kids really, but we were positioned as marketing experts inside the Toyota organization and had credibility because DFS was very highly regarded, plus we were fully backed by our executives and resources of the agency. We were also the only *gaijin* inside the Toyota organization at that time and became celebrities as we obviously stood out. We were pulled into all sorts of marketing and advertising projects, and were often required to compete against Dentsu, Hakuhodo and other Japanese marketing suppliers of Toyota. We usually won because we were much better at strategy and how to apply our thinking creatively to solve the business problems we were challenged to address. We became teachers of marketing (and English) and students of the *Toyota Way*.

Everything we worked on was directed outside of Japan. Europe, Saudi Arabia, Australia and Southeast Asia were the markets focused on in those days, while the DFS offices in the USA maintained their focus on Toyota USA. We were also asked to support a few one-off domestic Japan programs.

DFS was acquired by *Saatchi & Saatchi* in 1986; this had little impact on the Toyota team inside the agency as we were an agency-within-the-agency due to the size and scale of the Toyota relationship. But as a large global agency, and with *Yomiko* as our domestic Japan affiliated partner, we were pulled in to work on similar international marketing and advertising projects for Panasonic, Toshiba, Bridgestone, Seiko and other Japanese brands. Plus DFS/Saatchi had American and European clients in the Japanese market that we would occasionally help.

During my time in Japan, the country became the world's second largest economy, seemingly on the verge of taking over the entire world economically: the bubble era (late 80s) and the post-bubble era (two lost decades starting in 1991) leading up to the current *Abenomics* era. I married a Japanese woman from Tokyo in 1984; our two sons were born in Tokyo and I assimilated into Japanese family and daily life. BUT, I never forget that my added value in Japan is to always have an **outside** point of view and challenge the status quo.

In 2012, I and a group of fellow expatriate businessmen started to feel Japan was finished, its glory days behind it. We had enjoyed success in Japan and had remained optimistic during the two lost decades, believing the country would bounce back; and from time-to-time, we saw glimmers of hope. But it seemed the time had come to pack our bags and get out while we were still young enough to find work someplace else on the planet with brighter business prospects.

Japan suffered through the economic fallout of the Lehman shock and global depression 2008-2010. Just when things looked like they were getting better, the Great East Japan Earthquake struck on March 11, 2011, delivering a devastating blow to the economy and society. The yen peaked in the high 70s against the US dollar, hitting the export industries hard. There was a succession of weak prime ministers rotating through Nagatacho (location of Prime Minister's office). Tokyo failed to win the 2016 Summer Olympic bid. The consumer electronics industry lost its leadership to Apple, Samsung and LG Electronics. Japan had a declining and aging population, plus perpetual deflation. In December 2012 when Shinzo Abe was re-elected Prime Minister, based on his performance the first time he was in office, we figured this was the final nail in Japan's coffin and our expectations sank even lower.

But in 2013, Abe surprised us by exerting strong leadership and announced *Abenomics*. Tokyo's securing of the 2020 Summer Olympics was another vote of confidence. Japan is bouncing back and things are beginning to change. So I decided to stay and ride the next wave of opportunity. Japan is at an important *tipping point,* and I am betting on the upside.

Over the course of three decades as an advertising executive and marketing consultant working with Japanese companies, it was obvious from early on that most Japanese people have an imperfect understanding of marketing. The result is marketing that is not as efficient or as effective as it could be. Marketing does **not** have a core function in the Japanese business model. The *Chief Marketing Officer,* or CMO, position does not exist in Japanese business organizations.

I also believe Japan does a poor job of marketing itself to the outside world. The brand image of Japan is very strong and positive, but Japan fails to exploit it effectively.

I believe lack of marketing skill is a national competitive crisis as more and more Japanese businesses need to expand outside of Japan to survive or continue to grow. Marketing should be identified as one of the pillars of

Abenomics, as a critical item of national competitiveness to support key industries.

Marketing is an open area for Japanese women (*Womenomics*) to excel and build careers in; there is no glass ceiling in marketing, with management and board opportunities for rapid advancement.

Entrepreneurial start-ups, and small- and medium-sized companies need to develop marketing skills in order to grow by expanding outside of Japan.

The title of this book, *Make It Happen!*, was selected because that is exactly what Japanese business has to do, and I am challenging Japan's business leaders to elevate the role of marketing in their business. It is also the code I live by, as my personal and business reputation is based on *making things happen and getting things done* with the desired result. The ultimate evaluation for anyone in the business world is: *Are you a person who makes things happen*?

The world of marketing is going through dramatic changes due to the impact of the Internet and the vast amount of information instantly available 24/7; social media, the "Internet of Things", big data and the adoption of mobile smartphones as an essential appendage. This is having a rapidly evolving effect on the relationship between businesses and their outside agencies, no longer dominated by the advertising agency. Thanks to these innovations, marketers and businesses are better equipped with powerful tools to more effectively manage their marketing programs. Many businesses, especially in Japan, do not know how to make use of these tools; especially if they do not have a strong marketing foundation, resulting in missed opportunities and inefficient use of their marketing investments.

I believe there is a lack of understanding (or training) in marketing **basics** today. How can you execute Marketing 4.0 if you never learned Marketing 1.0?

Consider the military… Anyone who enters any branch of the military in any country, no matter what your position or rank, has to go through basic training, often called *boot camp*.

Basic training prepares recruits for all elements of service: physical, mental and emotional. It gives service members the basic discipline and tools necessary to perform the roles that will be asked of them. No matter which branch of the service a recruit chooses, basic training is an intense experience that teaches everyone to understand, respect and follow the chain of command.

No matter how old you are or how much experience you have, it is important to go back to the basics as your ultimate guide. Every person in a marketing job should have the same understanding of the marketing basics so that the entire marketing team is aligned and on the same page. Everyone should metaphorically know how to handle a rifle, load it, aim, pull the trigger and hit the target!

Make It Happen! is your ammunition. It is divided into the following parts:

1. An overview of the marketing function and why it is one of the most critical functions of business.
2. The six reasons Japanese companies struggle with marketing and my recommendations on what to do about it.
3. The basics of marketing (*boot camp*): I have stripped marketing down to its core elements through simplified explanations and examples. These are the basics for any business anywhere in the world to follow (with cultural adjustments). Japan needs to learn and apply these to compete globally.
4. Practical advice based on what I have learned in my career focusing on the marketing strategy and communications process inside a business and how to work effectively with outside agencies.
5. A check list to help you apply marketing basics to your business - a process to guide you through the questions you need to answer, which will help develop your marketing communications strategy.

6. Information about my life and career for those interested in learning more about me.
7. References to the books and materials I have used. If you want to dig deeper, any of these books are worth reading.
8. How to contact me if you need my help (three conditions involved).

If you are a business leader or work in marketing, this book should benefit you in the following ways:

1. You will know more than you do now about marketing.
2. You will be better prepared to do your job, make things happen and get things done.
3. You will be able to help other departments in your company understand what marketing does to improve cross-functional cooperation and overall business performance.
4. Your work will have a positive outcome, creating a sense of purpose and accomplishment.
5. You will (hopefully) be recognized and rewarded (along with your teammates) for a job well done.
6. You might discover you like marketing and wish to build your career around it and be curious to learn more.
7. You will have more confidence and courage to take risks, try new things and be an innovator to challenge those you work with to exceed expectations.
8. You will be able to share your knowledge and experience with those that follow you as a mentor and pass it on.

Finally, I would like to thank my son Robert, educated and working in marketing, for collaborating with me. At the time this book was written he was 29. His perspective on marketing is very different from mine. I come from the *Mad Men* world, while he is in the thick of the current marketing fragmentation driven by digital, social and mobile, and lives it in his daily life. He has helped me keep the content relevant while respecting my back-to-basics wisdom and experience.

My original mission when I arrived in Japan was to help Toyota improve its global marketing skills, and that mission is accomplished. My next and ultimate mission is to help Japan Inc. get better at marketing in order to secure the future global competitiveness of Japan. This book is a catalyst to provoke change and pave the way. The *Bob-san* nail will not be hammered down.[1] Consider me and this mission to be the *Black Ships* of marketing!

The author in Shimoda, Japan with a replica of Commodore Matthew Perry's flagship frigate, which was part of a squadron of American *Black Ships* that sailed into Tokyo harbor July 8, 1853, forcing Japan to end 250 years of isolation and open up to trade.

---

[1] There is a Japanese proverb that states, *"The nail that sticks up gets hammered down"*.

Dedication

To all my clients around the world, nothing would have been possible without you!

To all my friends and professional colleagues over the years, everything has been and always will be possible with you!

Special thanks to clients and friends at Toyota Motor Corporation since 1982: Yoshimi Inaba, Yoshio Ishizaka, Nobuyuki Sakurai, Konen Suzuki, Hiroshi Takada and Touri Ueno.

A debt of gratitude to wonderful mentors at Dancer Fitzgerald Sample (DFS): Rich Jahn, Jim Lindsey and Nelson "Skip" Riddle Jr.

In appreciation of Marietta College for everything I learned as a student and continue to experience there as an Executive-in-Residence.

To my wife, Yumi Kadoi Peterson, the best advisor any man could ever hope for.

PART 1

The Marketing Function

1. The Marketing Perception Gap Inside Companies

At the outset of writing this book, I thought it was important to define exactly what marketing is. After an extensive search, I could not find a definition that made any sense. Marketing has grown more complex over the years and is hard to define. Some companies are considering eliminating the word altogether and switching to the term *brand management* as an alternative.

Since I could not find a concise definition to open the book with, here is mine: *Marketing is a process to <u>persuade</u> the consumer to buy what you are selling.*

My son Robert, born in 1985, read this and immediately told me this is a 20th century definition. I asked him to help define marketing more suitable to 2015. He offered:

> *Marketing is the process involved to sell a product and brand. It addresses how a product or brand should be perceived by the customer to be more desirable (positioning); where and how it should be sold (selling & distribution); how to motivate purchases (value proposition & promotion); and how to serve and maintain the customer relationship (service).*

1

Marketing's goal is to bridge the gap between a product/brand and the customer by raising awareness, developing and managing relationships, and owning vehicles to reach them (e.g., communications and distribution channels).

Marketing is not an operations or business management activity. It does not involve product innovation, product planning, business strategy, new market identification, business analysis or sales forecasting; though it does play an important support role. Marketing produces a wealth of knowledge about the customer, products and market, and is important to consult while making better business and product decisions, and supporting related activities.

Marketers are the customer specialists, excitement generators, influencers, deliverymen and concierge that inform, attract, sell and ultimately take care of the customer.

Effectively managing marketing requires a strong understanding of the product/brand and the customer. All marketers must be able to answer five fundamental questions:

1. *What is the product/brand and what is its purpose?*
2. *Who is it for and why is it relevant to them?*
3. *How should the product/brand make the customer feel? What is the desired experience?*
4. *How, and through what vehicles, can that experience be realized, and what will motivate the customer to engage in a conversation and purchase?*
5. *Why should the customer believe you?*

While these questions are essential for all people within an organization to know, questions 4 and 5 particularly rely on marketers.

Thank you Robert!

The problem is that most organizations do not look at marketing this way. Marketing activities typically fall into two categories: Operational and Strategic. This is where I believe the disconnection comes into play.

The operational side focuses on the rational aspects of product management. Here is a list of tasks:

- Defining the competitive set
- Category attractiveness analysis
- Competitor analysis
- Customer analysis
- Market potential and sales forecasting
- Developing a product strategy
- New product decisions or modifications to existing product lines
- Pricing decisions
- Advertising and promotional decisions
- Channel management (where to sell)
- Customer relationship management
- Financial analysis and budgeting
- Marketing return on investment (ROI) measurement metrics

This operational list is how many people inside companies define what marketing does and what they do as *marketers*.
Operational work needs to be done to produce a product and determine how much of it can potentially be sold, where and at what price. When these tasks are completed, a marketing operations plan is produced. Then what?

Reach out to the intended customer (the prospect) and persuade them to buy. This is when marketing metamorphosis occurs: the product *caterpillar* transforms into the brand *butterfly*!

This requires a marketing communications strategy. This is the strategic or emotional side of marketing that manages brands.
Based on my experience, this is where many companies lack internal knowledge and experience. Under the marketing umbrella, the same

effort that goes into the operational side towards the product needs to go in the strategic and communications side towards the brand.

2. Importance of Marketing

Here is what Peter Drucker, an Austrian-born American management consultant, educator and author, whose writings contributed to the philosophical and practical foundations of the modern business corporation, has to say about the importance of marketing as quoted from his 1954 landmark book *The Practice of Management*:

"Because the purpose of business is to create a customer, the business enterprise has two – and only these two – basic functions: marketing and innovation. Marketing and innovation produce results: all the rest are costs. Marketing is the distinguishing unique function of the business."

"Marketing is so basic that it cannot be considered as a separate function. It is the whole business seen from the point of view of its final result, that is, from the customer's point of view."

Peter Drucker defined "marketing" as deeply understanding what the customer needs and values. It is not "advertising" or "selling," though many people in business may see it that way.

To orient everything around the customer in this manner was very much in line with his larger worldview.

Drucker's work carries over to religious, charitable, environmental, non-profit, social and governmental agencies, or any organization or group that has a particular cause to promote, needs to increase and retain membership or raise money. Just like a business, they also need to market themselves to achieve their goals. Political candidates need to market themselves to win their election. You need to market yourself to land the ideal job.

3. Marketing as Part of Company Strategy

Marketing is one of the two basic functions of the business. Therefore, a company's overall strategy needs to be reflected in its marketing.

Michael Porter is the Bishop William Lawrence University Professor at The Institute for Strategy and Competitiveness, based at Harvard Business School. He is a leading authority on competitive strategy, and the competitiveness and economic development of nations, states and regions. His work is recognized in many governments, corporations and academic circles globally. He is the author of 18 books and numerous articles. He is generally recognized as one of the intellectual leaders of the modern strategy field, and his ideas are taught in virtually every business school in the world. His work has also redefined thinking about competitiveness, economic development, economically distressed urban communities, environmental policy and the role of corporations in society. Drucker and Porter knew each other and collaborated at various times.

Porter's landmark book *Competitive Strategy,* first published in 1980, provides a framework for predicting competitor behavior that has transformed the way in which companies look at their rivals, and has given rise to the discipline of competitor assessment.

The following is a summary of his *five competitive forces* that directly impact a company's business strategy and thus, its marketing.

1. Current competitors
2. Threat of new competitors
3. Threat of substitutes for its products or services
4. Bargaining power of suppliers
5. Bargaining power of customers

Within the above environment, a competitive strategy must be chosen, and there are only three possibilities:

1. Achieving the lowest costs
2. Differentiating products and services
3. Dominating a niche

Trying to do some of each results in getting caught in the middle preventing the company from realizing the benefits of any of these strategies, and losing to competitors that chose just one.

To tie together Drucker's and Porter's work, a good example is Sir James Dyson, who invented the dual cyclone bagless vacuum cleaner that works on the principle of cyclonic separation. He created the Dyson brand, which disrupted an industry that was dominated for decades by Hoover and Electrolux. He freed consumers from inefficient vacuum cleaners in terms of cleaning performance, and eliminated the need to have paper or cloth bags that needed to be replaced inside the vacuum. He built 5,127 prototypes until he finally succeeded. He threatened an existing industry and succeeded by differentiating his innovation in vacuum cleaners through their unique design, performance and function. He did this through superior design (that also looks cool) at a premium price. His biggest resistance to gaining distribution came from the retail industry that made millions of dollars a year selling replacement vacuum cleaner bags. They were not keen to have Dyson's innovation kill this revenue stream. But consumers were willing to pay the premium to acquire a Dyson vacuum to free themselves of having to buy and change bags. His initial marketing campaign was built around the differentiating idea of *convenience* via the slogan, "Say goodbye to the bag!"

Since Dyson founded his company in 1983, consumers have voted with their wallets. His line of vacuums now dominates the global vacuum cleaner industry. He has expanded to challenge the fan and hand dryer industry by further innovating his cyclonic technology to eliminate the danger of fan blades, noise and choppy airflow. His hand dryers are eliminating the need for paper towels in public restrooms, saving trees and eliminating waste.

Meanwhile, Hoover, Electrolux and other vacuum cleaner brands may have recognized the threat, but were wholly invested in different technologies and a different business model, and continued to sell vacuums with paper bags as sales steadily declined. Retailers, having lost bag replacement revenue, are making up the difference through a greater range of Dyson products that sell at premium prices with better margins. Dyson's competitors have not found a strategy to respond other than to try and copy Dyson's technology and repackage it, and are now running into patent lawsuits.

Dyson has invested in marketing campaigns globally that are consistent in its approach, focusing on product function and design that deliver the benefit of superior cleaning performance and convenience. What was once an uncool, low-interest product category is now cool, and consumers are willing to pay a premium to have a Dyson.

4. Marketing within the Company Structure

Every business was once a small business. Some grew to be become massive global corporations, and some went bankrupt or broke up and faded away with changing times. Every business, large or small, public or private, *Business-to-Consumer* (B2C) or *Business-to-Business* (B2B) is a mini-nation, city, village or family. They go through various stages. Each has its own history, culture, management style and reason it exists. Marketing plays a key role in the success, sustainability or failure of every business.

The CEO or owner of the business should be directly involved in the marketing. Why? Because as Peter Drucker stated, *"Marketing is the distinguishing unique function of the business."*

Depending on the size of the business, the CEO should appoint a Chief Marketing Officer (CMO) or assign one of his senior officers to be responsible for marketing (e.g., Director of Marketing reporting directly to the

CEO). This person should have a seat on the board or management committee. Finally, marketing should be recognized as a core function of the company and work cross-functionally in equal partnership with the other parts of the company.

Professor Philip Kotler of Northwestern University in the USA, often referred to as the "Father of Modern Marketing" and author of numerous marketing books, took part in the *World Marketing Summit Japan* 2014. He was interviewed by Nikkei journalist Atsushi Sato and asked to comment on his belief that businesses need a CMO in charge of a company's marketing. What attributes does Professor Kotler think are required of a CMO? He responded as follows:

"There are two. First of all, creativity. This is because CMOs have to produce big ideas, or have special insight (into the consumer). The other is the ability to collect data, analyze it and develop insight. An ideal CMO should not only have creative insight, but also the capability of being a leader who produces ideas and foster future leaders too."

In Japanese companies the CMO position does not exist and marketing is not considered a core function of the business. This is out of line with Drucker's and Kotler's thinking. In the USA, where the position is common in most companies, CMOs have a high rate of turnover or burn out.

I believe the CMO position has grown too complicated for one person to manage and needs to be expanded to a broader group of people to function as a CMO team.
Considering Professor Kotler's view that there are two key requirements for a CMO, creativity is a right-brain function, while data analysis is a left-brain function. The right-brain, left-brain theory originated in the work of Roger W. Sperry, who was awarded the Nobel Prize in 1981. According to the right-brain, left-brain dominance theory, the right side of the brain

is best at expressive and creative tasks. The left-side of the brain is considered to be adept at tasks that involve logic, language and analytical thinking.

It is extremely difficult to find a CMO qualified to know every aspect of marketing and have both sides of their brain working in perfect balance.

Additionally, the amount of data being generated is overwhelming due to the proliferation of media platforms. In addition to basic market share and sales data, CMOs are confronting nine key categories of *Big Data* as defined by *Advertising Age,* the industry's leading publication:

- Mobile data
- Customer relationship management (CRM) data services
- Social media marketing and analytics
- Campaign measurement and digital analysis
- Data management platforms
- Offline-to-online data onboarding
- Predictive analytics (marketing mix modeling)
- Shopper and loyalty marketing
- Cross-channel marketing

Since CMO is an abbreviation that universally signals the marketing function in a company, my suggestion is to redefine and rename it the **Customer Marketing Office**.

A team of executives working collaboratively, each responsible for different marketing functions, with a rotating team captain (who speaks directly to the CEO and other board members). This allows for a variety of talents to meet Professor Kotler's requirements when their collective brain power is focused together to balance strengths and weaknesses.

This spreads out responsibility and pressure so it is NOT all dependent on one *superman.*

Together, the members of the CMO act as the voice of the customer and represent them inside the company.

A team approach is more flexible to permit response to rapidly changing competitive challenges, shifting consumer trends and the impact of *Big Data.* Planned rotations allow for a constant inflow of new thinking while retaining wisdom and experience; thus, marketing is integrated into all company functions as an equal team player. The Customer Marketing Office will lead and mentor the internal marketing organization and be supported by specialist outside agency partners. They establish key performance indicators (KPIs) to measure return on investment (ROI) for marketing expenditures and define what success should look like to justify marketing expenditures to the Chief Financial Officer (CFO). They also report directly to the business owner or CEO, who has to take ultimate responsibility for managing the company brand.

Marketing needs to work cross-functionally and in partnership with the other key functions of the business leading to the customer. This means the mindset of everyone in the organization has to be one of sharing and working collaboratively in an open and honest way. The charts on pages 11, 12 and 13 are my recommendation of how marketing fits into the overall company business organizational structure, breaks down into various functions and works cross-functionally. This can be modified and adapted to fit company size and product range.

The first chart shows the basic functions of any business; scalable to the size of company operations and number of employees. The Customer Marketing Office is established as its own function separate from sales.

Basic Organizational Structure

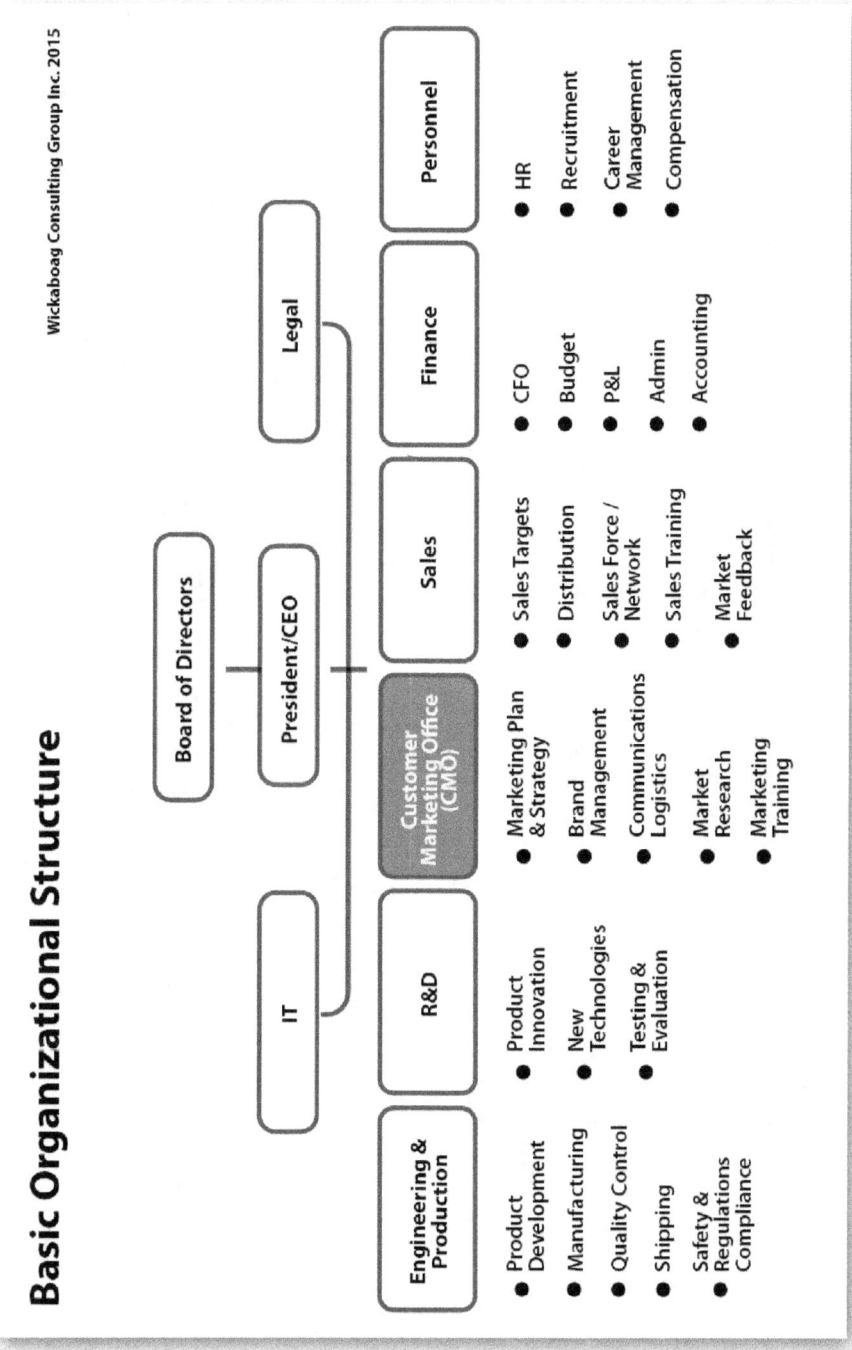

Wickaboag Consulting Group Inc. 2015

Board of Directors

President/CEO

IT

Legal

Engineering & Production
- Product Development
- Manufacturing
- Quality Control
- Shipping
- Safety & Regulations Compliance

R&D
- Product Innovation
- New Technologies
- Testing & Evaluation

Customer Marketing Office (CMO)
- Marketing Plan & Strategy
- Brand Management
- Communications Logistics
- Market Research
- Marketing Training

Sales
- Sales Targets
- Distribution
- Sales Force / Network
- Sales Training
- Market Feedback

Finance
- CFO
- Budget
- P&L
- Admin
- Accounting

Personnel
- HR
- Recruitment
- Career Management
- Compensation

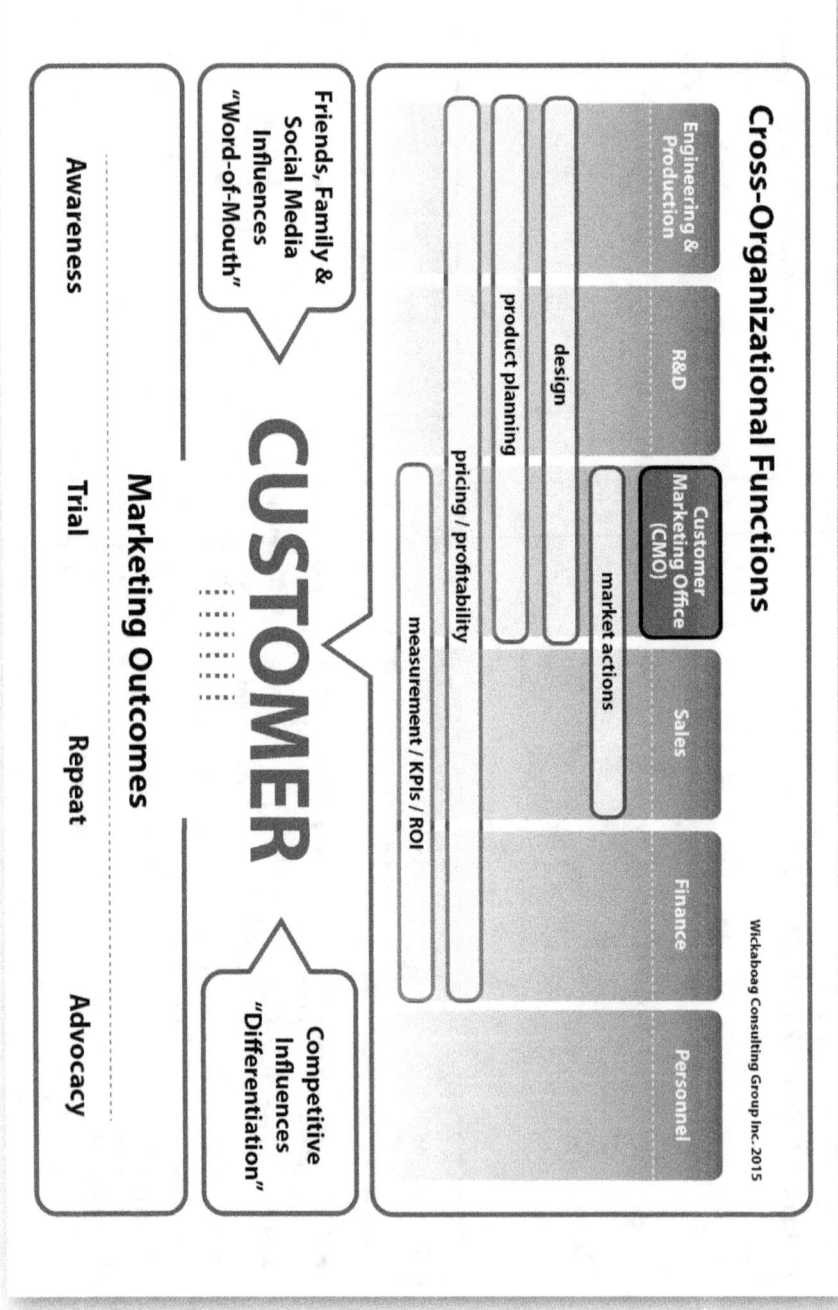

CMO Structure & Marketing Functions

Wickaboag Consulting Group Inc. 2015

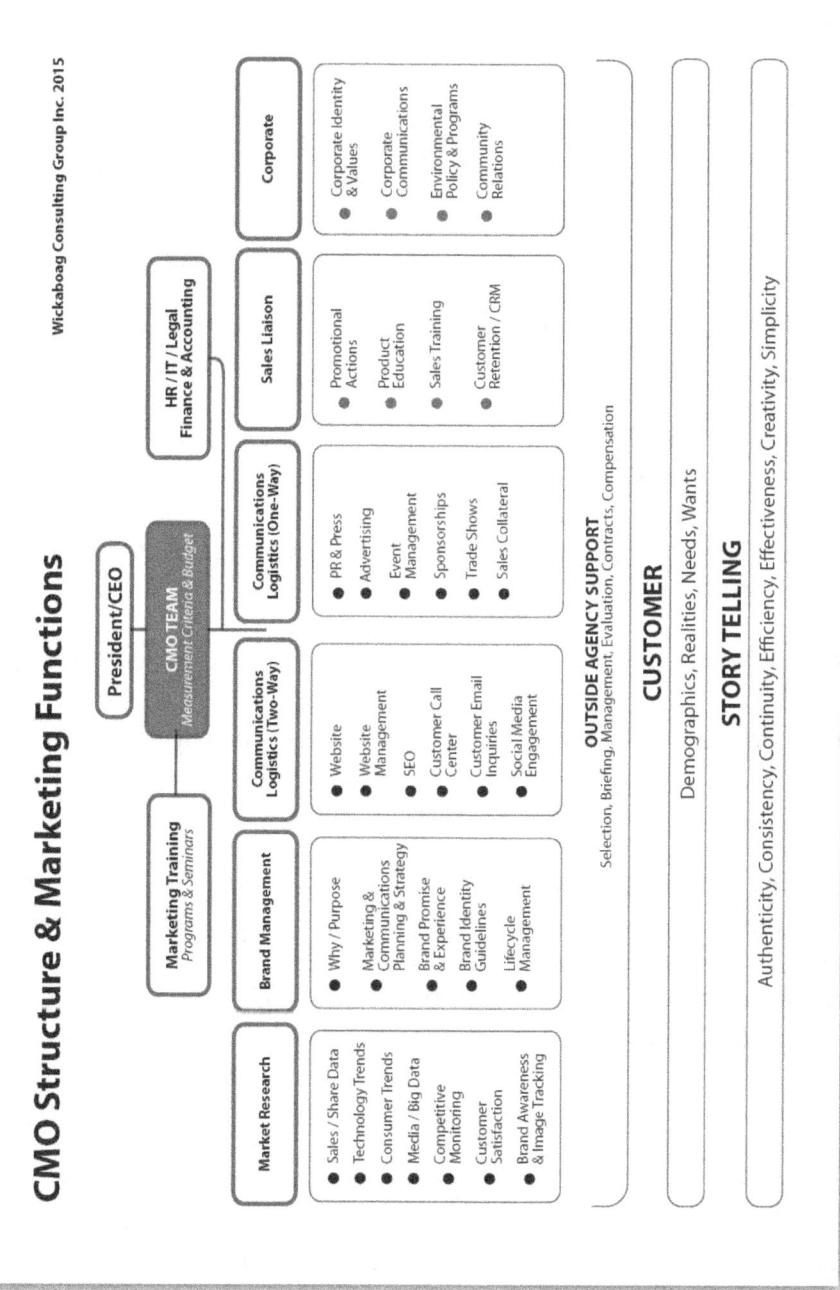

President/CEO

CMO TEAM
Measurement Criteria & Budget

Marketing Training
Programs & Seminars

**HR / IT / Legal
Finance & Accounting**

Market Research
- Sales / Share Data
- Technology Trends
- Consumer Trends
- Media / Big Data
- Competitive Monitoring
- Customer Satisfaction
- Brand Awareness & Image Tracking

Brand Management
- Why / Purpose
- Marketing & Communications Planning & Strategy
- Brand Promise & Experience
- Brand Identity Guidelines
- Lifecycle Management

Communications Logistics (Two-Way)
- Website
- Website Management
- SEO
- Customer Call Center
- Customer Email Inquiries
- Social Media Engagement

Communications Logistics (One-Way)
- PR & Press
- Advertising
- Event Management
- Sponsorships
- Trade Shows
- Sales Collateral

Sales Liaison
- Promotional Actions
- Product Education
- Sales Training
- Customer Retention / CRM

Corporate
- Corporate Identity & Values
- Corporate Communications
- Environmental Policy & Programs
- Community Relations

OUTSIDE AGENCY SUPPORT
Selection, Briefing, Management, Evaluation, Contracts, Compensation

CUSTOMER
Demographics, Realities, Needs, Wants

STORY TELLING
Authenticity, Consistency, Continuity, Efficiency, Effectiveness, Creativity, Simplicity

The chart on page 12 shows how the Customer Marketing Office interacts with the other key functions of the business, and where they have to overlap and work cross-functionally. The combined actions are aimed at the customer. The customer is most influenced by two key factors: on the right, the need to differentiate from the competitors; and on the left, family, friends and social media that have a powerful *word-of-mouth* influence on how the customer thinks and acts with their wallets. This flows into the four marketing outcomes, which are explained in the next section.

The chart on page 13 breaks down the Customer Marketing Office responsibilities. At the outset, the CMO Team needs to set the criteria by which all marketing actions and investment will be measured. It also has the ultimate responsibility to convince the CEO and CFO to approve the marketing budget.

The next layer down breaks marketing into six functional areas; the boxes are self-explanatory.

These functions are supported by a variety of outside agency partners.

The collective output is the story you want to tell the customer.

5. Four Outcomes of Marketing

Jim Stengel, former global Chief Marketing Officer of Procter & Gamble, currently President/CEO of the Jim Stengel Company and Adjunct Marketing Professor at UCLA's Anderson School of Management, teaches these *Four Outcomes of Marketing* to his marketing MBA students.

Awareness

If your target customer does not know your product exists or where to buy it, you are out of business. So the very first thing you need to do is figure out how to create awareness and maintain it over time.

Trial

Once the target customer has found your product and has decided to buy it for the first time, it is the ultimate *moment of truth*. Did it meet expectations? If the answer is no, your business is in trouble. If the answer is yes, move to the next point.

Repeat

You have a satisfied customer who likes your product and appreciates its perceived value. You now have a chance to build an ongoing relationship so they continue to purchase.

Advocacy

Not only does this customer *like* your product, but also they are probably interacting with your customer service people, engaged with your marketing messages, activities and offers, and they have joined your *Facebook* page or other social sites and enthusiast groups. They are telling their friends and family via *word-of-mouth,* which can be further amplified by social media, blogs, etc. This is the *Holy Grail* of marketing. Don't screw it up!

Most marketing books teach that marketing is the 4-Ps (product, price, place and promotion).

I believe Jim's four outcomes are more relevant and actionable.

The example I used earlier about Sir James Dyson and his line of innovative vacuums, fans and hand dryers is a good demonstration of achieving these four outcomes.

6. Help the Consumer to Become Your Customer!

Consumers today face a plethora of choices and are bombarded daily with hundreds of competing offerings fighting for their attention to *buy*.

Make it easier for consumers to tune into a brand's marketing message and transform them into customers. Please follow, and always remember, these two basic principles when planning and evaluating marketing communications.

K.I.S.S. = *Keep It Simple Stupid*

This is an important consideration when formulating the marketing strategy by *searching for the obvious*. An obvious strategy is simple, easy to understand, evident and powerful. *Common sense* is your guide; it is wisdom shared by all. Simple ideas tend to be obvious ideas because they have a ring of truth about them.

W.I.I.F.M = *What's In It for Me?*

The questions every consumer asks themselves when confronted with any communication about a brand is, "*Should I take a moment to listen or read, engage and respond? What is in it for me?*" Has the brand helped them with the answer as they go through the decision process before turning over their hard earned money?

PART 2

Why Japanese Companies Struggle With Marketing

In November 2012, Jim Stengel was in Tokyo as a special guest speaker for a conference a major Japanese ad agency was holding with its senior clients; the topic relating to the Chief Marketing Officer. The intent of the conference was to encourage Japanese companies to adopt the CMO system. As I mentioned earlier, CMOs do not exist in Japanese companies.

I invited Jim to our home for dinner with my wife, Yumi. We had a lovely evening and discussed what Jim just experienced at the conference, our assessment of the *Toyota Brand Forum* program we worked on together in 2010 and 2011, and a general discussion about Japanese companies challenges' with marketing.

Yumi listened to and participated in our discussion. Later that night, she reminded me that there is no word in the Japanese language, no kanji, for marketing. It is a foreign word with no direct translation and could be one of the reasons Japanese have a hard time understanding what marketing is. Yumi's comment sparked me to think more deeply about why Japanese companies struggle with marketing, and I decided to figure out what other reasons there might be.

I put myself in the position of a doctor examining and treating a patient. I determined the *disease* had not been diagnosed properly: outside *gaijin* experts like me trying to help Japanese companies with marketing had been treating the symptoms and not the underlying cause of the disease itself. All my efforts working with Japanese companies up to this point were nothing more effective than an aspirin or a bandage. From November 2012 to April 2013, I developed a white paper on the topic, and eventually turned this into a series of articles and presentations starting in 2013. So far my point-of-view has received wide acceptance and no push back.

In April 2013, I began the process of reviewing my white paper with Japanese business executives, friends in the Tokyo marketing community and Professor Taro Kamioka Ph.D., Graduate School of Commerce and Management, Hitotsubashi University. Kamioka-sensei (i.e., Dr. Kamioka) has a deep interest in marketing, and in particular, the CMO function. He researched the topic for a book he wrote, including interviewing Jim Stengel when he was global CMO of P&G. He agreed to review my paper and eventually we met to discuss it. He received my paper in advance and noted his comments in little balloons. One comment jumped out at me and helped confirm that I was on the right path: *"Marketing in Japan plays only a small role in corporate decision-making."*

1. Six Reasons

Following are the six reasons I believe Japanese companies struggle with marketing.

1) Language

In the Japanese language, there is no direct translation for the word or concept of *Marketing*. It is spelled phonetically via five *katakana* characters (separate alphabet for foreign words): Ma-Ke-Ti-N-Gu.

The word *marketing* contains the word *market*, and this is where the confusion is believed to come from. The English word *market* has been assimilated into the Japanese language and communicates a place to shop or to *make a sale*. When the Japanese hear the word *marketing*; they appear befuddled as their ears hear only *market*, the *ing* has no meaning. The mind jumps to a sales transaction taking place in a market.

This is one reason why, in Japanese companies, *sales and marketing* are connected together as if they are the same function. Sales activities represent 80-90% of their efforts; marketing is limited to actions to support sales.

The Japanese language is brilliant for negotiating intricate social relationships, preserving nuances and saving face. It is not known for clarifying thoughts or fostering open and honest debate, which tough marketing decisions require.

2) Cultural history

Monozukuri, *Mono* (thing) and *Zukuri* (process of creating, producing, manufacturing with a high level of craftsmanship), is a relatively new Japanese word. It combines the desire to produce excellent products with the ability to constantly improve productions systems and processes. This underpins the Japanese business economy. The drivers of *monozukuri* and business direction are the product engineers. Marketing staff have a lower status in the organization.

This ties back to the Tokugawa shogunate government, which intentionally created a social order called the four divisions of society (*Shi-no-ko-sho*) that stabilized the country in the Edo period (1603-1868). Classes were arranged by what Confucian philosophers described as moral purity.

1. *Samurai* (*shi*) are at the top of society because they set a high moral example for others to follow.
2. Farming peasants (*nō*) come second because they produce the most important commodity, food. According to Confucian philosophy, society could not survive without agriculture.
3. Third are artisans and craftsmen (*kō*), producers of material goods.
4. Fourth, and at the bottom, are the merchants (*shō*), because they generate wealth without producing any goods.

In today's corporate Japan, this *caste system* continues: engineers are the samurai, factory workers are the farmers, suppliers are the artisans and craftsmen, and sales and marketing staff are the merchants.

3) Education

Marketing is taught based on its operational and theoretical applications in Japanese universities; not from the strategic or emotional side of marketing that manages brands. It is not a major or field of career specialization. University professors do not have professional, practical experience in marketing compared to some professors in American or European universities where marketing is offered as a major for career specialization at the undergraduate and MBA levels. Japanese companies do not have marketing training programs.

4) Talent management

Employees are rotated through marketing during their career; it is not an area of career specialization. When an employee is placed in a marketing position they have to figure it out on-the-job, and it does not matter what their level or rank is. They do not have mentors or knowledgeable managers to guide them. There can be an overreliance on outside suppliers to help, such as the advertising agency to help them fulfill their assignments. Experience gained is rarely retained and passed on to the next person rotated in to fill the position. Aptitude for a marketing position is not a consideration. Executives and staff in marketing positions have not had basic training in the fundamentals of marketing.

Marketing is not represented at the board level as a core function of the business; the CEO does not always appear to be directly involved in the company's marketing. In today's highly competitive *war-like* marketplace, marketing is too critical to be left to middle-level generalists as a tactical function to support sales. Since marketing is not considered a core function of the business, management does not want to undermine their departmental employees in a bottom-up organization; they want to give them full responsibility. This feeds a perpetual cycle of marketing mediocrity. That results in tremendous inefficiencies, poor accountability and measurements, and continuing to do what has always been done in the past. In Japan, no one wants to risk being first; going second is more comfortable as someone has cleared the path.

5) Lack of incentives

There is no incentive or reward to try something new and different. There is a fear of change: it is better to imitate or continue with the status quo. *Ringisho** or *nemawashi** ensures bold strategies are rarely pursued. There is a preference in Japanese culture for consensus and harmony. If anyone dares to risk trying something new or different and it does not work, they will most likely be punished or even black-listed, possibly bringing an end to their career. There is no sense of professionalism or pride in output.

**Ringisho* means *a high-level formal authorization/approval process*.
**Nemawashi* means an informal process of quietly laying the foundation for some proposed change or project by talking to the people concerned, gathering support and feedback.

6) Tactics vs. Strategy

Japan's business strategy from the 1960s onward was to focus on high quality at a competitive (lower) price. The practices and approaches Japan pioneered in doing so changed competition around the world forever.

Japan's approach to marketing has followed these tactics: growth at the expense of profitability, proliferation of products and features, continuous operational improvement confused with strategy (a means to an end), serve all market segments, sell through multiple channels (everywhere), emulate competitive approaches and the customer is God. This means every customer is equally important no matter how much they spend! Additionally, understanding and articulating what a brand is and how it should be managed is a mystery.

To compete on strategy, Japan has to learn to compete applying unique positioning involving a distinct product offering, achieving operational effectiveness and differentiation, and performing the same or similar activities better than competitors. Everything must be measured and requires real innovation (not just quality improvements). Making tradeoffs and choosing what not to do require constant discipline and clear communication to guide the organization.

Finally, Japan needs to move beyond just quality competition to competing on quality <u>and innovation</u>. Genuine innovation not only in products, but also in approaches to competing is required (e.g., marketing).

2. Apple iPod vs the Japanese Electronic Company's Easy Carry XVZ-22R

When Sony's Akio Morita directed his engineers to create the Walkman in 1979, he launched a revolution in the way people listen to music. A little over 20 years later, Apple founder Steve Jobs reinvented the portable music player with the innovative *iPod*.

Jobs launched his game-changing product with the slogan: *"iPod. One-thousand songs in your pocket."*

In one simple phrase, Mr. Jobs also told us *why* we wanted the *iPod*! The Apple brand had already conditioned us to *Think Different* and believe anything from Apple had a *cool* factor to it. Up until the *iPod* launch, Apple was just a computer company. Consumers easily accepted a personal music player from this computer company. Apple backed up the *iPod* with the *iTunes* store so we could load it with songs at a reasonable price immediately. Consumers ran out and bought it; technical details, features and price were secondary considerations.

I imagine a Japanese electronics company, having invented the same product, might have presented it something like this:

> *"Today we are introducing a new, portable music player called the Easy-Carry XVZ-22R. It weighs a mere 6.5 ounces, is about the size of a shirt pocket, and boasts voluminous digital capacity, long battery life, and lightning-fast transfer speeds. We will be introducing many variations of the Easy-Carry XVZ-22R that incorporate different functions and feature different colors."*

The Japanese company (probably the engineer who developed it) presenting the *Easy-Carry XVZ-22R* as a competitive response only told us what it did and how. There was no emotional connection or reason for us to believe it was a better product at a lower price that could also download songs via the Internet. The brand making it had a reputation for high quality, reliable products. A piece of hardware that inspired no one working on its marketing nor the consumer.

Steve Jobs, through a simple single phrase, established the key benefit; he did *not* speak to consumers like an engineer with lots of technical terms and statistics. Apple has since taken Japan by storm with the *iPhone* and *iPad*. Meanwhile, Sony (and many other Japanese electronics companies), in the post-Morita era, is struggling to figure out its future; especially in the audio-visual field on which it built its global brand reputation.

3. Implications and Recommendations

Embracing marketing as a core function of the business does work **inside** Japan. Coca Cola, P&G, McDonald's and Starbucks, among many other Western companies, have entered the Japanese market with entirely new brands and product categories (with cultural adjustments) and were accepted by Japanese consumers. Japan is a growth market for Apple, and Dyson recently entered Japan with its line of vacuums and fans. Both brands are supported by compelling innovation and marketing stories consistent in the companies' global approach.

Many of these non-Japanese companies are leaders in their categories. Japanese companies have created *copy-cat* competing offerings with varying degrees of success.

All of these outside brands recruited and trained Japanese managers in their marketing methods with great success. Many of these well-trained and experienced Japanese marketing professionals have jumped ship to traditional Japanese companies with the ambition of applying their marketing knowledge and skills. But most have only experienced frustration and regret by hitting a brick wall of resistance for the reasons noted above. What a tragedy.

A few Japanese companies have progressive CEOs who understand the importance of marketing as a core function of the business and have fully embraced it by adopting American-influenced marketing systems and methods. This has allowed them to successfully expand their businesses globally. What works in Japan works very well in Japan, but not always outside Japan.

These are my recommendations to Japanese business owners and CEOs who desire to implement marketing as a core function of the company's business:

1. Separate sales and marketing into two distinct functions and clarify the role or mission of each.
2. Create a Customer Marketing Office/CMO function reporting directly to the CEO, elevated to board-level function. The CEO must be directly involved!
3. Rearrange the company's organization and working processes to build in the CMO function.
4. Elevate the status of marketing in the company; allow employees to specialize or develop a career in marketing as a skilled profession.
5. Introduce an ongoing marketing recruitment and training program with outside help.
6. Treat your outside agencies as partners, not suppliers; they advise, you decide!
7. Implement a process to measure the ROI, effectiveness, efficiency, consistency and continuity of marketing investments, and *kaizen* everything through defining your KPIs.

8. Build in incentives and rewards for the CMO team and outside partners.

If Japanese CEOs can convince their management team and board of directors to embrace the Customer Marketing Office/CMO function, the result of fully embracing marketing as a core function can help companies to:

1. Maintain or regain innovation leadership.
2. Hit sales goals and build market share with better margins.
3. Increase brand value in the mind of the customer (and within the financial community).
4. Have a motivated and focused company organization aligned behind a clear marketing and communications plan and strategy.

I have invested over 30 years of my life and career supporting Japanese companies' marketing efforts. It has often been frustrating in an indefatigable effort to help my clients improve their marketing. But for every step forward, I have often experienced two steps back due to the fact marketing is not seen as an important function in the company, combined with a constant turnover in the marketing department, resulting in a complete lack of professionalism. The CEO is preoccupied with areas of the business deemed more important to focus on.

The future of Japanese business lies outside Japan as the domestic market shrinks due to the low birthrate and rapidly aging population. Japanese CEOs and their management team must figure out the best way to elevate marketing in their company and establish the Customer Marketing Office/CMO function as a solution. Japanese companies need to expand outside of Japan to grow. Marketing is essential to make this happen.

Japan needs more progressive CEOs to be marketing champions. The future success of Japanese businesses and all the people they employ around the world are dependent on this vital change from business-as-usual practices. Someone needs the guts to be first!

If Japanese companies cannot shift their thinking, a 21st century remake of Hollywood movie *The Last Samurai* might be titled, *The Last Engineer. A man of great moral purity... but few customers.*

PART 3

The Strategic Basics Marketers Need to Know, Never Learned or Forgot

1. Building a Solid Strategic Foundation

Before any building is constructed it needs a solid foundation or it will eventually collapse. It is the same with marketing communications: a strategic foundation must be built or it will be ineffective and waste money.

Before building construction begins, a careful study needs to be made of the underlying soil conditions and location of bedrock, analysis of transportation inflow and outflow, access to utilities, fire and safety regulations, extreme weather considerations and building code regulations. Excavating the site, placing the pilings or footing, forming and pouring the concrete foundation, and hooking up to the utilities is hard, dirty, tedious, time-consuming and monotonous work; but it must be done first and with absolute precision. No corners can be cut. Once the foundation is in place, the building on top of it rises quickly to take on any form or function the architect designed it for. Some buildings take on iconic status and become key landmarks and establish a unique identity for the place it is built (e.g., Eiffel Tower). Every building needs a foundation, and the same basic principles apply underlying how it is constructed.

A solid strategic foundation will lead to an effective and efficient marketing communications program.

One of my earlier ambitions in life was to be an architect. I have had a lifelong fascination with building and construction. My two grandfathers were engineers: one an MIT graduate and the other a self-taught Swedish immigrant. I was lucky enough to live in private suburban homes growing up. Every Saturday, my father and I started the day with a trip to the hardware store, lumber yard or garden center to buy what we needed for the project of the day. My father taught me how to fix and make just about anything around the house as well as take care of the lawn and garden.

This carried over to our family summer home on Lake Wickaboag in West Brookfield, Massachusetts; a 2x4 wood-construction summer cottage built by my great-grandparents on the side of a small hill overlooking the lake. It was passed on to my grandmother, my father's mother. In the early 1970s, the house was over 50 years old and in need of serious work to save it. This became my amateur architecture project. During my high school drafting classes, I drafted detailed drawings of the cottage, designed a new bathroom addition, a remodeling plan for the kitchen, new outside decks and plans for additional rooms under the house.

The problem at the outset was that the cottage sat on wooden posts over bare dirt; there was no basement. Additionally, the posts were rotting and causing the cottage to sag and settle unevenly. Eventually the cottage would collapse. I had my summers free between 1972 and 1975 while I attended Marietta College and decided to do all the work on the house during these summers as an ambitious project through my own initiative. Of course, I wanted to start with the fun stuff, building the new bathroom, remodeling the kitchen, decks, etc. But my father said no, it would be a waste of time and money with no foundation under the house. So he told me to put a foundation under the house first and then start the other things in my architectural master plan. My grandmother agreed to support the project, approved my plans, and put up the funding for the materials and equipment if I was serious about doing the work.

The outer dimensions of the cottage are roughly 10 x 14 meters. The front of the cottage is about 2+ meters above the ground, the back sitting on the ground. Starting in the summer of 1972 and finishing in the summer of 1974, with the occasional help of my younger brother and cousins, I excavated by hand all the dirt under the cottage (pick ax, shovel and wheel barrow), devised a system to put sections of the cottage on temporary jacks, poured concrete footings and built cement-block walls over 2 meters high. I taught myself masonry, bricklaying and the engineering to level the cottage. As sections of the walls were built, the cottage was lowered onto the new wall, jacks moved and the process repeated section by section until the entire exterior of the cottage and interior supporting beams sat on cement-block walls. Some of the outer supporting wood beams were rotten and had to be replaced too as we went along. The new basement was planned to add additional bedrooms and storage, with exterior access and a new interior stairway to the main floor. In total nearly 2,000 cement blocks were used.

With a solid foundation in place, during the summer of 1975, the new bathroom addition was built, kitchen remodeled, new outside decks added and rooms built in the basement. This used all my skills as a carpenter, electrician, plumber and interior designer.

I am very proud to report that 40 years later the cottage foundation has not shifted or settled one millimeter, with no cracks in the cement-block foundation walls. The family continues to enjoy the cottage every summer. By conducting periodic maintenance and updating, we will continue to do so for many generations to come.

The same applies to your marketing program; build a good, solid foundation first! What follows in the next sections are the building blocks of your marketing communications strategic foundation.

2. Start with WHY?

The first question to answer is, **_Why_** _does your brand exist?_

Simon Sinek's presentation on _How Great Leaders Inspire Action_ is the third most viewed video on TED.com. His 2009 book on the same subject, _Start With Why: How Great Leaders Inspire Everyone to Take Action_, delves into what he says is a naturally occurring pattern, grounded in the biology of human decision-making, that explains why we are inspired by some people, leaders, messages and organizations over others. Simon calls this the _Golden Circle: Why, How, What. "People don't buy what you do. They buy why you do it."_

What: Every organization on the planet knows what they do. There are the products they sell or the services they offer. This relates to the neocortex part of the brain that controls analytical and rational thinking plus language. This is where you prove what you believe at the center of the _Golden Circle._

How: Some organizations know how they do it. These are the things that make them special or set them apart from their competitors. This relates to the limbic part of the brain that determines feelings, trust and loyalty; it has no basis for language. This is where decision-making and gut feelings (i.e., sometimes something does not feel right and we cannot explain why) come from.

Why: Very few organizations know why they do what they do. Why is not about making money. That is a result. Why is a purpose, cause or belief. It is the very reason your organization, product or brand exists. This is also part of the limbic brain function that controls emotion, behavior, motivation and long-term memory affecting decision-making. Companies that can explain what they do from the inside out create belief among customers by believing in why they do what they do.

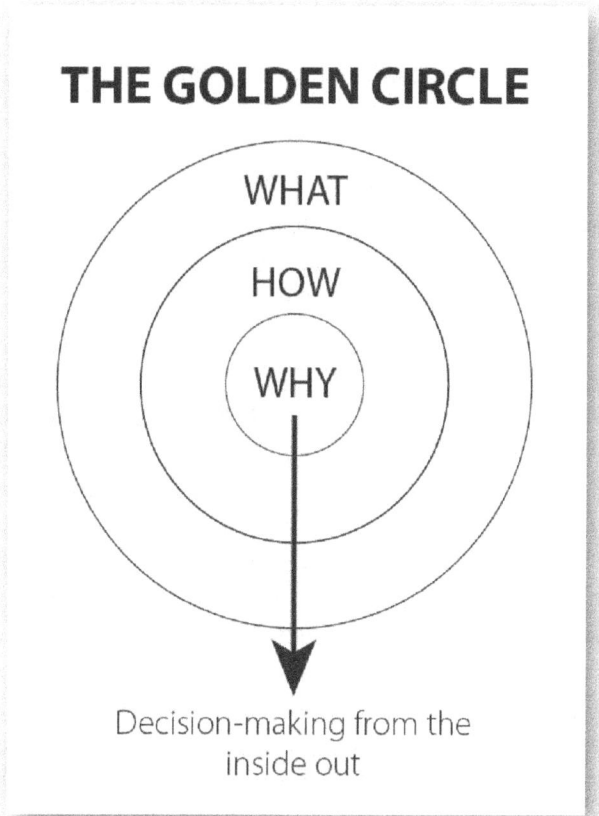

THE GOLDEN CIRCLE

WHAT

HOW

WHY

Decision-making from the
inside out

Carrying this over into the marketing communications strategy helps focus other elements of the plan, and inspires everyone working on the project how to think, act and communicate with the customer.

3. Brand, Branding, Brand Management

Every company or product has a name; that name is the *brand* (which should be copyrighted or trademarked).

Some companies put their name on their products (e.g., Toyota). Some companies make a range of products with different brand names (e.g., Procter & Gamble).

Branding helps the customer to easily identify the company and its product and distinguish them from its competitors. People use brands as a short cut or filter to make purchase decisions. A brand is what the company or product stands for in people's minds; it can be a feeling or an image.

To the customer a brand *is a promise wrapped inside an experience.*
An important exercise every brand goes through is determining what it is promising the customer based on their realities, wants and needs.

The brand *experience* is what the customer sees, feels and responds to at every point of contact with the brand, including the marketing. If the experience is delivering a level of satisfaction that meets or exceeds customer expectations, and if they are passionate enough, they may be willing to share this with family and friends. These customers are your *brand champions* and become fiercely loyal. If they encounter anything negative that causes them to lose faith or be turned off, they can become *brand terrorists*, and broadcast their grievances or just switch to a competing brand. Customers ultimately vote with their wallets.

David Aaker is the E.T. Grether Professor Emeritus of Marketing Strategy at the Haas School of Business, University of California Berkley and Vice Chairman of Prophet. Professor Kotler refers to David Aaker as the "Father of Modern Branding." In the past, he has served as an advisor to Dentsu, a major Japanese advertising agency. He has written over 100 articles and 15 books; his six books on branding have been translated into 15 languages.

One of David Aaker's greatest contributions to branding goes back to the late 1980s when the idea emerged that brands are assets, have equity, and drive business strategy and performance. This altered perceptions of marketing and the role of marketing executives. More and more executives realized that tactical brand management (just pushing short-term sales) was inadequate, and a strategy-led brand vision, plus organizational processes combined with skills to implement and measure that vision, were critically needed.

Leading on brand strategy requires the marketing role to be elevated in the organization with the CEO being the ultimate brand champion. Marketing is a core function participating in creating and managing the business strategy. The elevation of marketing and brand building as a driver of business strategy provides a point of entry for the CMO team. Once in place, marketing has much to offer to business strategy development, starting with customer insights that can and should enable growth initiatives, and be the basis for strategic resource allocation.

David Aaker is the creator of the *Aaker Model*, a marketing model that views brand equity as a combination of brand awareness, brand loyalty and brand associations. The model outlines the necessity of developing a brand identity, which is a unique set of brand associations representing what the brand stands for (its *promise*) and offers to customers an aspiring brand image (via the *experience* it is wrapped in). Aaker primarily sees brand identity as consisting of various elements which fall under four perspectives:

- *Brand as Product* – consists of product scope, product attributes, quality or value of product, uses, user and country of origin.
- *Brand as Organization* – consists of organizational attributes and local workings versus global activities.
- *Brand as Person* – consists of brand personality and customer-brand relationship.
- *Brand as Symbol* – consist of audio and visual imagery, metaphorical symbols and brand heritage.

Brand Equity is a phrase that describes the value of having a well-known brand name, based on the idea that the owner of a well-known brand name can generate more money from products with that brand name than from products with a less well-known name or private label: Consumers believe that a product with a well-known name is better than products with less well-known names.

A brand can lose its value quickly if a company has a major product recall (Toyota's 2009-2010 stuck accelerator controversy in the USA sparked a global quality crisis), causes a widely publicized environmental disaster (British Petroleum's 2010 oil spill in the Gulf of Mexico) or makes a change to the product that its loyal customers do not accept (*New* Coke via *Old* Coke in mid-1980s).

All brands go through a lifecycle, starting with the day they are launched into the market. These are the three brand lifecycle phases that become **brand management**:

Launch – A brand has achieved the four outcomes of marketing, congratulations! A massive short-term effort has been made by the entire organization to pull this off; heavy upfront investment, awareness and interest have been successfully generated. It has been a steady ramp-up or a surprise hit and now the brand has reached cruising speed.

Sustaining – This is the most challenging marketing job; keeping it going under the assumption the brand is making a healthy financial contribution (i.e., profitable). The brand has to generate its own revenue to sustain its supporting marketing program. This is a delicate balancing act: continued investment is needed to stay competitive and sustain sales. Underspending or *milking-the-brand* to fatten the company bottom line can lead to its decline.

Metaphorically comparing a brand to a train: First, securely hitch all the cars together so they are ready for the intended destination. It takes a tremendous amount of energy (fuel) to get the train moving up to its sustainable speed. A train travels with a certain rhythm and inertia; it is not easy to stop once it gets going. Depending on the type of train and tracks, it can be traveling at a high rate of speed, like the Japanese *shinkansen*, or at a slower sustained speed like that of a commuter or freight train. The engineer pays careful attention to all signals and track conditions ahead to avoid a collision or derailment. Occasionally, the train needs to stop for refueling, maintenance or to pick-up or drop-off passengers and cargo, but the train returns to its journey. However, what happens if the engine is unhooked from the cars? The engine pulls away and fades into the distance, the cars clickity-clack along for a while, but eventually slow down and come to a stop, dead in the tracks. The passengers and cargo are marooned. This is what happens when a company fails to continue to invest in their brand's innovation and marketing. Moving a stalled train takes more time and money to get it moving again, especially if it derailed in the process. Tell this story to your CFO to avoid a train wreck.

Decline/Reversal/Death – Due to changes in consumer tastes and trends, competitive actions, or whatever the reason, customers are not buying the brand anymore, sales and share are in decline. At this point, the marketing team has to consider the following:

- Are innovations possible to improve the brand's point of *differentiation* and attempt to re-launch it as *new and improved*?
- Is there something that can be done with marketing communications in terms of strategic message, creative approach or media spending that can reverse the trend?
- Pull back marketing support, keep supplying loyal customers (as long as there is enough demand) and *milk-the-brand* until it is no longer profitable, and then pull it off the market or sell it.

Brand management becomes complex when multiple products are sold under the same brand name. Toyota sells a wide range of models all with different names. Toyota becomes the *master brand*, the various models become *sub-brands*. The Toyota master brand represents *quality, reliability* and *durability* (rational) providing the customer with *peace-of-mind* (emotional). The model sub-brands benefit from the master brand power as they sharpen their marketing strategy against their direct segment competitors.

Many companies use the power of a product's brand image and market share power to add line extensions that offer consumers more options to satisfy micro needs while maximizing sales and profit potential and defending against competitors.

For example in laundry detergent, a brand has captured a dominant share of the market with only one product (in various sizes) that delivers on the promise of making clothes *as-clean-as-clean-can-be*. New innovative competitive products begin attacking this brand. The company responds by innovating and launching additional product variations under the same brand name related to bleach additives that make clothes even whiter, or color guard protectors, or the ability to clean in cold water (to save the utility cost of generating hot water), or to be more efficient by cleaning in less water, or adding various fragrances. These are called brand line extensions, and begin to stretch the core brand promise and experience.

What was once a simple task for the customer to clean clothes with their familiar favorite brand becomes a much more complicated decision-making process due to having to decide which one of all these new brand product variations to choose from, some maybe at premium prices. Some loyal customers will welcome this increase in choice, and trust that the brand will continue to deliver on its promise and accept increased prices. Some others may be confused and turned off by too much choice, and switch to a competitive brand that offers a simple choice with a similar brand promise at an affordable price. Did these brand extensions expand, or at least protect market share and profitability while increasing production, packaging and marketing costs due to adding all of the other variations under the same brand name?

All branding decisions come with risk as the persuasion techniques aimed at human buying motivations are not a black-and-white science. We have to make some educated guesses and roll the dice to see what happens in the marketplace.

4. Differentiation

For a brand to be successful it must *differentiate* itself from the competition in the mind of the prospect, and this difference must be relevant. This helps the prospect make choices among competing offerings, and provides key information to determine points of superiority, parity or deficiency. This results in a *unique selling proposition,* or *USP.*

When consumers are facing a decision about what to buy, they are making an evaluation based on their realities, wants and needs. Income, savings and access to credit is a reality that plays a major factor in what consumers can afford.

Food is one of the most basic things we need every day to survive. When looking at the range of food choices, we start from the most basic things we need to live and stay healthy such as fruit, vegetables, meat, dairy products, and bread, and then widen the range to items like candy or snack foods which taste and make you feel good but do little to sustain life. Luxury goods may be something you want to have to look good and impress others but do not necessarily need to live, or are out of your price range all together.

Whether it is food or luxury goods, there is a range of brands to choose from at all price points. Be clear where your brand fits on the scale of the customers realities, wants and needs and their purchase motivations.

Identify the direct competitors as well as similar products in the category. In other words, places where customers flow toward the brand or places they could flow away from it. Consider the drinks business. If brand A offers a natural 100% fruit juice drink, it is competing with other natural 100% fruit drinks. While 100% fruit drinks may be seen as the healthy choice, they also have a higher price point. But when the consumer is making a decision about a fruit-flavored drink (or anything to drink when they are thirsty), they may also consider all types of fruit drinks that are not natural and are not made from 100% fruit, which may cost less. They could also be considering sports or carbonated drinks. Even plain water! It is important to take a broad view when evaluating the competition.

The competitive analysis should include the following:

- Current sales and market share – trends
- Research on consumer trends that are relevant to the brand's product category
- Intense understanding of everything about the brand compared to its competitors – advantages and disadvantages
- Marketing communications audit
- Consumer research related to brand image and levels of customer satisfaction
- Summarization of strengths, weaknesses, opportunities, threats (SWOT) analysis

If you do not know your enemy, you can neither win the battles nor the war; they are certainly waging war against you!

Jack Trout has more than 40 years of experience in advertising and marketing. He is the author of many marketing classics which I have listed in the reference section of this book. He is the champion of *differentiation.*

He published an article in Forbes magazine on July 3, 2006, called *Tales From The Marketing Wars - Peter Drucker On Marketing.* I have kept it on file as a useful reference, and share here Jack's thoughts on the importance of **differentiation** in the marketing wars.

To become a great (marketing) strategist, you have to put your mind in the mud of the marketplace. You have to find your inspiration down at the front, in the ebb and flow of the great marketing battles taking place in the mind of the prospect. Here is a four-step process:

Step 1: Make Sense In The Context
Arguments are never made in a vacuum. There are always surrounding competitors trying to make arguments of their own. Your message has to

make sense in the context of the category (your brand is competing in). It has to start with what the marketplace has heard and registered from your competition.

What you really want to get is a quick snapshot of the perceptions that exist in the mind, not the deep thoughts.

What you're after are the perceptual strengths and weaknesses of your brand and your competitors as they exist in the minds of the target group of customers.

Step 2: Find The Differentiating Idea
To be different is to be not the same. To be unique is to be one of a kind.

So you're looking for something that separates your brand from the competitors. The secret to this is understanding that your differentness does not have to be product related.

Consider a horse. Yes, horses are quickly differentiated by type. There are racehorses, jumpers, ranch horses, farm horses, wild horses and on and on. But racehorses are differentiated by breeding, by performance, by stable, by trainer and so forth.

Step 3: Have The Credentials
There are many ways to set your company or product/brand apart. Let's say the trick is to find the difference and then use it to set up a benefit for your customer.

To build a logical argument for your difference, you must have the credentials to support your differentiating idea, to make it real and believable.

If you have a product difference, you should be able to demonstrate that difference. The demonstration, in turn, becomes your credentials. If you have a leak–proof valve, then you should be able to have a direct comparison with valves that leak.

Claims of difference without proof are really just (empty) claims. For example, a "wide-track" Pontiac must be wider than other cars. British Air as the "world's favorite airline" should fly more people than any other airline. Coca-Cola as the "real thing" has to have invented colas.

You can't differentiate with smoke and mirrors. Consumers are skeptical. They're thinking, "Oh yeah Mr. Advertiser? Prove it?" You must be able to support your argument.

It's not exactly like being in a court of law. It's more like being in the court of public opinion.

Step 4: Communicate Your Difference
Just as you can't keep your light under a basket, you can't keep your difference under wraps.

If you build a differentiated product, the world will NOT automatically beat a path to your door. Better products don't win. Better perceptions tend to be the winners. Truth will not win out unless it has help along the way.

Every aspect of your communications should reflect your difference. Your advertising. Your brochures. Your web site. Your sales presentations.

5. Positioning
This is an exercise to put the brand into the mind of the prospect. That is, positioning the brand in the mind of the prospect. It is how the brand differentiates itself in the mind of the prospect.

In 1994, the American Chamber of Commerce Japan held an event featuring Stephen R. Covey; he became famous through his book, *The Seven Habits of Highly Effective People*. Over his lifetime, Stephen traveled the globe many times over. His message was a simple one: for true success and meaning in life, we must be principle-centered in all areas of life.

The Tokyo luncheon event was packed with a large cross-section of American business expats. Stephen started his presentation wandering through the audience asking us to imagine that we had died but we were able to observe our funeral and listen to what family, friends and colleagues are saying about us. Then he asked, are they saying what you would expect or hope they would be saying? My marketing interpretation of this is, **if they are,** then you positioned yourself well in life and all your actions supported that positioning. Your funeral is your final confirmation! **If they are not** saying what you would expect, then you must ask yourself why?

Stephen then moved into the core of his recommended principles that we should live by. His presentation had a profound effect on me and I took his words to heart and started thinking about my funeral.

Positioning the brand correctly will help avoid the funeral altogether.

6. Three Types of Communications

Marketing communications provides vital information to customers enabling them to find or discover the brand to make an informed buying decision. There are three types of communications to manage:

One-way – Work the brand creates: directs its creation, approves it, places it in the media, pays for it and controls it 100%. This is advertising (TV, radio, press, outdoor) or direct marketing. It is an effective and efficient way to build awareness. Consumers know this is coming directly from the brand and can be skeptical about its contents. This is what brands did prior to the late 1990s when the Internet started to change consumer communications dynamics.

Two-way – Open communication channels via the Internet that give the customer the opportunity to participate and respond to the brand's marketing communications directly 24/7 as well as broadcast their opinions to anyone who cares to listen. These are websites, social media, blogs, live engagement or experiential events, special interest consumer groups, *YouTube* videos, photo sharing sites, etc. Other than the planning, production and management of the brand's website, social media pages or event site, there is little or no control over how consumers respond and decide to *share*. But it needs constant monitoring. It is a delicate balance of managing *brand champions* vs. *brand terrorists*! This is currently referred to as *digital, social, mobile* and now dominates marketing and advertising activities.

Public Relations (PR) – The consumer will seek out independent third party sources, primarily in the press, for assurance and confirmation during the shopping process to help support a purchase decision. Consumers seek out and trust what professional journalists or experts (influencers) write about. These sources decide if the brand is worthy of coverage, positive or negative. Trying to manipulate or influence these sources is risky. It is best to deal with them openly and honestly. Sources are no longer limited to physical newspapers or magazines, all are instantly accessible via the Internet.

7. Single-minded

If we pack too many messages into the brand marketing communications, the prospect is not likely to remember anything, or be confused. Sometimes the brand only has a few seconds to engage the prospect to get their attention keeping in mind K.I.S.S. and W.I.I.F.M. Developing a strong, strategic single-minded USP and bringing it to life in a compelling way is rooted in the genuine understanding of the realities, wants, needs and motivations of the people who use the brand.

Here is a way to visualize this.

You and I are standing about three meters apart. I pick up a tennis ball and toss it directly at your face with little warning. You will instinctively put your dominant hand up to protect it and firmly catch the ball as a reflex reaction. I now have your full attention and you'll want to know why I tossed a tennis ball at you. You accept my reason at face value (because you know and trust me), or perhaps with some skepticism (what is he really up to?), and we move on.

Now what happens if I toss two tennis balls at you? You might catch one and deflect the other.

Let's keep increasing the number of tennis balls I toss at you, and eventually you can't catch any of them. Some may hit you in the face and cause some minor pain. Now the balls are rolling all over the floor and you are starting to get angry and upset. Finally, you turn your back on me and escape. You are not likely to ever play with me again.

The same thing will happen when too many, or conflicting messages are tossed at the brand's prospects. Provide one clear message and supporting points or reasons to believe and the prospect will respond accordingly.

8. Defining the Target

The brand needs to define its target customers from two perspectives. These are:

Demographics – Sex, age, occupation, interests/hobbies, education, income and location. Facts that can help the brand determine the potential size of the group to calculate sales and profit potential. But it does not reveal anything about how they think or feel as individuals.

Psychographics – Realities, wants and needs. Put yourself into the shoes of the brand's prospect and the situation in which they will use or interact with it. The brand's marketing must fit into their realities, the most basic of which is affordability. As noted above, you have to consider where the brand fits in their scale of wants and needs. Is the brand is something they really need or just something they want? Go through an imaginative writing exercise to describe the brand's prospect as a person, not a statistic. This is critical to guiding the creative process supporting the brand's marketing communications.

9. Customer Purchase Cycle

Consumers purchase brands at different intervals. New cars are purchased at intervals of 3-7 years, clothes are purchased seasonally, cleaning products as they run out, and food daily. Knowing where the brand sits in the customer purchase cycle has an impact on the strategic plan, communications and marketing actions.

At Saatchi & Saatchi, we used a diagram to show the four phases of the customer purchase cycle. We adapted this to Toyota and I have continued to use it ever since in my consulting work. Below is the Toyota diagram; it is self-explanatory and can be easily adapted to any brand.

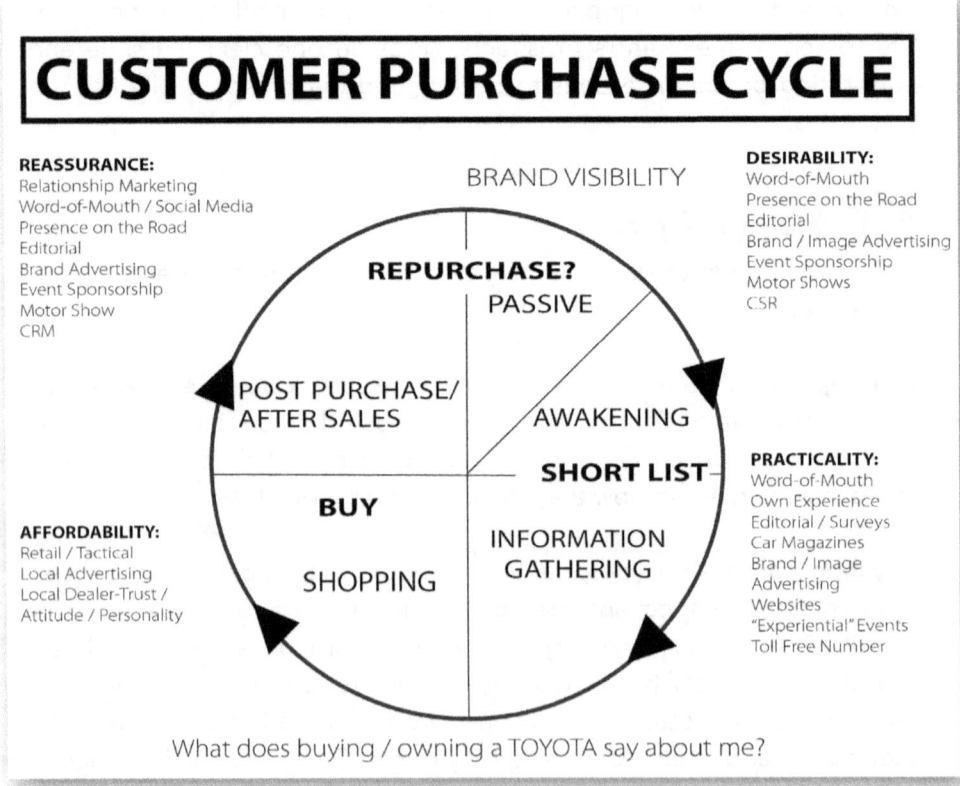

CUSTOMER PURCHASE CYCLE

REASSURANCE:
Relationship Marketing
Word-of-Mouth / Social Media
Presence on the Road
Editorial
Brand Advertising
Event Sponsorship
Motor Show
CRM

BRAND VISIBILITY

DESIRABILITY:
Word-of-Mouth
Presence on the Road
Editorial
Brand / Image Advertising
Event Sponsorship
Motor Shows
CSR

REPURCHASE?
PASSIVE

POST PURCHASE/
AFTER SALES

AWAKENING

SHORT LIST

PRACTICALITY:
Word-of-Mouth
Own Experience
Editorial / Surveys
Car Magazines
Brand / Image Advertising
Websites
"Experiential" Events
Toll Free Number

BUY

INFORMATION
GATHERING

AFFORDABILITY:
Retail / Tactical
Local Advertising
Local Dealer-Trust /
Attitude / Personality

SHOPPING

What does buying / owning a TOYOTA say about me?

10. Media Planning

Today, media drives the output of the marketing communications process.

A little over a hundred years ago, society had few sources of mass information. Travel was limited to the privileged few by ocean liner, train and the beginning of the automobile industry. Beyond what you heard via word-of-mouth in the area where you lived and worked, mass information was available through newspapers, magazines, outdoor posters, and sporting or spectacle events (e.g., traveling circus) that gathered large crowds - public address systems were not used yet either. These were the channels through which brands used to be marketed to consumers. But even with these limited channels, marketing communications still needed a foundation. The points covered in this book applied then, as they continue to do now.

What has happened over the past hundred years is a proliferation of media channels and the speed to get and share information.

In the 1920s and 30s, it was the development and influence of radio, movies (first silent, then talkies, B&W and color) and the public address system.

In the 1950s, B&W television reached homes via analog terrestrial signals, starting a steady stream of innovations up to the present: color broadcasting, cable and satellite distribution, channel proliferation, the transition to digital signals, time-shifting due to VCRs and TIVO, tube TVs evolving to plasma/LCD flat screens of ever-increasing sizes, and tablets and smartphones.

In the 1980s, direct marketing became another channel for marketers to reach consumers in a highly targeted way.

All this was one-way communication paid for by the marketers. The only real means for the consumer to express their opinions back to sponsoring brands was with their wallets, or if they were passionate enough, by writing a letter or telling their limited circle of friends and family. Occasionally, the press would pick up on a story if a particular brand was a big sensation (iPhone) or was a threat to the public's well-being (environmental disaster).

In the late 1990s, the impact of the Internet arrived starting with websites, blogs and e-mail. Since the turn of the century, we have witnessed the rise of Google, Facebook, Yahoo, a stream of Apple products, Skype, YouTube, Twitter, Apps and many, many more. People who never before had a voice now have one, and they can communicate to the whole world with immediate impact and influence. There has been a massive explosion of media channels, which brands have no control over. Companies can control the content they pay to produce and load into all these channels, but not how people choose to use it, adapt it, share it, time shift it and talk about it.

Brands are adapting to this brave new world where they are engaged in a 24/7 dialogue with their customers. This makes managing the output of marketing communications much more complex. But it still needs a strategic foundation. A hundred years ago, buildings were only a few stories high in New York City, now we have skyscrapers all over the world.

Up until this transition point, ad agencies would come up with a creative *big idea* and then adapt it across TV, radio, print, outdoor and direct marketing. As TV was the dominant media channel, if a brand could afford it, TV was the ideal media as the core of a marketing communications program. Public relations always seemed to play a *second fiddle* or supporting role.

Brands now need to do an in-depth analysis of what media channels their target prospects and current customers are most influenced by. Before starting the creative process, a brand has to determine its media plan first. If the brand requires mass advertising, the creative process might be led by TV and then adapted across other media channels. If the target is a very narrow niche and best reached through web channels, then the creative process will need to web-based or any combination in-between.

Public relations are much more important, and in some situations, may lead the marketing communications program.

Brands need to master the art and science of **communications logistics**; that is, total communications planning from the premise that all communications with the customer are *speaking with one voice*, giving one message rather than fragmenting in different directions.

These are some basic media terms to be familiar with. It is vital that a brand's marketing communications **reach** the target group with enough **frequency** to achieve its intended objectives. The brand also needs to consider its **share-of-voice (SOV)** in the media against its competitors.

If the brand has four competitors (in its market niche), then all five together have a combined market share and media spending equal to 100%. It is highly unlikely that each has 20% market share and 20% SOV in media spending. If brand A has 50% market share, it probably has a SOV of between 40-60% that helped it build up its market share and is now keeping it there.

If brand B has a 10% market share and its SOV is at or below 10%, and its objective is to increase its market share to 20%, it may have to increase its SOV disproportionately to 30% or more to achieve it.

If brand A drops its SOV to 20%, there is a danger its market share will drop due to less awareness in the market.

The agency responsible for media can calculate what the media spending level should be vis-à-vis the brand's objectives and target. This is called a **task plan**. The agency will provide an analysis with supporting data to indicate the level of media spending and across what channels to balance effectiveness with efficiency. They should provide several options highlighting the pros and cons of each with a clear recommendation. Then it comes down to a decision on budget allocation and what the brand can afford to spend.

There is no point in going through the time and expense to produce marketing communications if they are not seen in the right media channels enough times to have the desired effect.

11. Importance of Story Telling and Slogan

Story Telling

Long before the advent of mass communications, people sat around the fire and told stories to entertain each other or pass on vital information from generation-to-generation. People today still love a good story. Marketing communications planning is preparing the story a brand wants to tell.

The best book I have read about this is Seth Godin's *All Marketers Tell Stories*. I have summarized Seth's key points as follows.

If you hope to sell anything, concentrate on the story you tell in your marketing. The story you tell affects the way your prospect feels about your brand.

The story, when you come right down to it, **is** the brand.

Some consumers will avoid or resist or deny your story. That's okay. Tell your story to people who want to hear it, who want to believe it, who will tell their friends. A good story (either from the marketer or the customer) is where genuine customer satisfaction comes from. It's the source of growth and profit and it's the future of your organization. Successful marketers are just the providers of stories that consumers want to believe! Everything and everyone has a story. The key is how you tell it with authenticity, consistency, transparency, robustness and frame it within the world of your customer's realities, wants and needs.

Slogan

Developing a slogan, memory mnemonic device or musical jingle/signal for a brand helps get the attention of the prospect; with repeated exposure over time it becomes memorable. It should have stickiness and indicate the type of product and/or benefit. It becomes an essential element of the brand identity. To the internal organization, it can serve as a battle cry or call to action. Two well-known examples are Nike's *Just Do It* and Apple's *Think Different*.

12. Measurement - Setting Benchmarks

To evaluate the effectiveness and efficiency of a brand's marketing communications, it is important to determine how to measure success based on the following four areas:

1) **Objectives** – These should be more than just sales and market share goals. They need to state the business issues the marketing communications are to address. While it is important to be ambitious and *shoot for the moon*, they should also be within the realm of being realistically obtainable.

2) **Outcomes** – *War game* from the best case to the worst case scenarios. Create a vision of what success will look and feel like.

3) **Key Performance Indicators (KPIs)** – These measure real-time sales and market share data, customer feedback/dialogue and behavior shifts, efficiency of the working process and any number of other measurable factors.

4) **Return on Investment (ROI)** – This is to determine the effectiveness of marketing investments. It is always of keen interest to the CFO.

These four measures serve as a *kaizen* process – continuous improvement and feedback to measure progress and to guide adjustments. They should not be used as a weapon to punish the marketing organization if management is not happy with the results. Establishing open, unbiased measurement criteria at the outset will also minimize wishful or delusional thinking.

Success (as well as failure) should be celebrated and rewarded: we often learn more from failure than repeated success. Nothing goes up forever, and unforeseen circumstances such as *Acts of God* or being blindsided by unanticipated competitive actions can never by fully anticipated. The marketing organization should be prepared and flexible enough to deal with any eventuality that is not in the actual plan. The marketplace is a fluid, constantly changing battlefield.

One of the challenges the marketing team faces is the massive amount of data to work with, and how to interpret and apply it without becoming lost and confused.

13. Why Was Apple So Good At Marketing While Steve Jobs Was Alive?

Apple is the gold standard when clients and agency people are asked to give an example of a great marketer. When this question comes up in conferences or discussions, Apple is always mentioned. It appears to be universally accepted that Steve Jobs was the genius behind Apple's growth to become the most valuable company in the world. Steve was not an engineer, nor a finance guy. Steve, above all else, was a great marketer.

Apple co-founder, Steve Wozniak, told the BBC, "*I would say marketing was his greatest strength.*"

Steve knew the basic fundamentals of marketing, always stayed true to them and built a solid marketing communications foundation set deep into bedrock. Above that was built the most valuable brand name in the world. He also had a deep partnership with Apple's ad agency, TBWA.

Just after Steve Jobs died on October 5, 2011, *Advertising Age* published an article on October 7 paying tribute to him titled *STEVE JOBS WAS A*

DIGITAL MAVERICK BUT A MARKETING TRADITIONALIST - Steve Jobs revolutionized computing and media, but when it came to marketing he was a bold traditionalist.

Here are the key points edited from the article:

- At a time when marketers obsess over the virtues of targeting "likes," dashboards, platforms of all stripes and sophisticated social-monitoring schemes, Mr. Jobs kept it simple: tell the story of how an amazing product can change your life in the best environment possible.
- While many accept the lessons of Mr. Jobs the product designer, and have sought to emulate him in that regard, it seems they all too often overlook his influence as a marketer, where he was decidedly – and effectively – old school (basics).
- Mr. Jobs was involved in every aspect of the marketing, down to the copy in the TV ads.
- Mr. Jobs produced at least two of the finest TV ads of his generation, and ubiquitous billboards and magazine ads. In later years, demo videos of Apple products went viral.
- "Every great brand needs investment and caring if it is to retain its relevance and vitality," Mr. Jobs said to his staff after he returned to Apple in 1997 and unveiled the "Think Different" campaign. The scene was caught on tape and fortunately preserved for history on *YouTube*.

So why don't more companies think about marketing like Steve? "Too much is pulled into tactics with a lack of meaning and strategy," says Jim Stengel. "The tactics and the meaning have to come from leaders, and there are too few of them out there."

14. Intel Inside®
To put all of these blocks together with an example, I have selected Intel. Intel makes computer chips, something we never see inside our computers and most consumers have no idea what they do, how they work and

don't care about them. They are a commodity. But Intel has made us care via a brilliant marketing campaign rooted in a solid foundation and managed with consistency and continuity for over 20 years.

Intel was founded in 1968 and built a reputation for high-quality and reliable microprocessors. Microprocessor sales is a highly competitive market, confusing to consumers and the products are seen as a commodity.

In 1991, Intel decided it needed to differentiate itself from its competitors and build a consumer brand. Intel believed it could position its microprocessors as a premium product, which it could in turn sell at a premium price to computer manufacturers. To give computer manufacturers and their retail customers a reason to identify Intel in their marketing, Intel chose to market its product as a branded component.

Intel convinced manufacturers that their computers would have higher perceived value if they featured Intel in their own marketing. That meant creating brand awareness for Intel chips in computers amongst the manufacturers' direct customers (the dealer) and the end-user (consumers and corporate purchasers). The first step was to commit Intel to a fully integrated brand strategy. They chose to invest in "ingredient" branding – the creation of equity as an input brand (a computer chip brand inside a computer brand). Another example of this is NutraSweet, Monsanto's brand, an artificial sweetener used in thousands of food and beverage brands.

In 1991, Intel launched a co-op program in which they convinced manufacturers to place the "Intel Inside®" logo in their advertising, on their packaging and products, plus in other marketing materials.

The brand name "Intel Inside®" became the first trademark in the electrical component industry. This campaign focused the entire organization around the brand and created a highly effective advertising campaign. The Intel Inside® campaign aimed to "educate both the retail sales associates and the consumers about the value of Intel microprocessors

(W.I.I.F.M.), and to explain to them the differences between microprocessors", without technical jargon (K.I.S.S.).

Many consumers were uncertain about the quality and reliability of microprocessors, and Intel found a way of taking away the mystery of the product, and gaining the confidence of the end user that Intel Inside® represented quality and reliability.

Intel's advertising campaign generated awareness for itself, and then went a step further via a bright idea of contributing to computer makers' campaigns through co-op funding as long as they promoted Intel Inside® at the same time.

The advertising results were stunning. For example, late in 1991, Intel research indicated that only 24 percent of European computer buyers were familiar with the Intel Inside® logo. By 1995, it had soared to 94 percent and continues at this high level today. According to Interbrand's 2014 *Top 100 Global Brands* survey, Intel ranked as the world's 12th most valuable brand, valued at $34.2 billion (Apple is #1, valued at $118.8 billion). The Intel Inside® innovative branding and marketing program made this happen (backed by outstanding microprocessors of course).

Computer manufacturers began co-branding their computers with the Intel Inside® logo and indicating which generation of microprocessor was used, thereby creating sub-brands (e.g., Atom™, Centrino®, Core™, Pentium®). Intel Inside® has gained wide recognition, and consumers perceive it as a benefit in performance.

Consumers now look for Intel Inside® when they buy computers. If they don't see the now familiar logo, they are likely to wonder, "Why don't they use Intel chips? Are they using something cheaper or not as good?"

With its ingredient branding program, Intel raised awareness for both microprocessors in general, and preference for its own microprocessor brand in particular. Suddenly, consumers and business decision-makers alike considered what was hidden deep inside the computer before making a purchase, and Intel provided a relevant solution meeting customers realities, wants and needs at an affordable price.

This is my interpretation of the Intel Inside® story based on the above strategic building blocks:

Why does Intel exist?
To make your computer run reliably and fast.

How does Intel do it?
By putting state-of-the-art, high-quality microprocessors inside your computer.

What does Intel do?
It makes microprocessors backed by constant innovation and the highest possible manufacturing standards.

What is Intel's brand promise?
High-quality, reliable, fast microprocessors.

What is the Intel brand experience?
Trouble-free and responsive (processing speed) computer usage.

What is Intel positioning against competitors?
Highest quality, most reliable, most advanced, fastest microprocessors preferred by OEMs, retailers and consumers.

What is its single-minded message?
Intel Inside®

What is the Intel story?
Intel Inside® makes a difference.

What is Intel's use of media?
- In 1991, started out as one-way media.
- Point-of-sale and product packaging.
- Expanded and adapted to *two-way* media by adding web, social and digital communication channels.
- Backed by heavy spending budget to achieve reach and frequency to build/maintain awareness plus a dominate SOV.

What is the Intel slogan and brand ID?
- Intel Inside® logo
- Intel Inside® jingle
- See Intel website for detailed Intel Inside® brand ID and usage guidelines.

KPIs
- Achieved all objectives and outcomes
- 90+% awareness of Intel Inside®
- Dominant market share
- OEM, retailer, customer preference

ROI
- Brand and stock market valuation
- Premium pricing

An interesting twist to this story is that Intel Inside® was created and first used in Japan as *Intel Haitterru* (i.e., literally *Intel in it* in English) and adopted globally.

PART 4

Practical Advice

This section is to share practical advice I have learned over the course of my life relevant to my professional activities.

I have lived in Rochester and New York City in New York; Fairfield and Stamford in Connecticut; Allentown, Pennsylvania; Cleveland, Ohio; Los Angeles, California; Miami and Palm Beach Gardens in Florida; Manila, Philippines; Mexico City, Mexico; Tokyo and Nasu, Japan; Brussels, Belgium; Rome, Italy and at Lake Wickaboag in West Brookfield, Massachusetts. I have been blessed with the gift of traveling to many places around the world.

Starting in my teenage years and continuing until graduating from Marietta College in Marietta, Ohio, I worked in construction, house painting, landscaping, theatrical lighting and stage design, acting, TV and radio production, radio announcing and food service. I know what it is like to get my hands dirty and what it takes to earn a dollar through hard work.

My professional career started with selling toilet paper, paper towels, disposable baby diapers and facial tissue for P&G in New York City supermarkets. I worked for several famous global advertising agencies in client and strategic management for major brands in oral care, hair care, cleaning products, tapes and adhesives, automotive, electronics and fast food in the USA, Japan and Europe.

I have managed and worked with diverse groups of people from supermarket clerks to creative directors, art directors, copy writers, market researchers, strategists, TV commercial directors and production houses, photographers, printers, web designers, event planners, a range of people in media, engineers, translators, interpreters and clients at all levels in their organizations.

I have managed multinational teams in Japan and Europe, worked on national, regional and global advertising campaigns overseeing dozens of TV commercials and print ads, brochures, events and sponsorships. As a consultant, I also learned to work with small- and medium-sized companies that are family or privately owned in a variety of industries, as well as governmental organizations, educators, journalists and editors.

When I started working in the late-70s, my working environment included an electric typewriter, rotary dial telephone, telex and snail mail. I have easily adapted to everything that has happened since in business and communication technologies, and consider myself *tech savvy*.

Marketing is dominated by young people, so I am always around young people. They challenge me to stay sharp, young-at-heart and seem to like having me around to mentor them. Most recently, I am learning how to share my wisdom, experience and opinions as mentor, lecturer and author.

Over this diverse range of multicultural, multilingual work around the world, I always kept running into the same problems and frustrations that get in the way of getting things done efficiently and effectively, or throw the work off course resulting in a waste of time and money. I have broken these down into the four areas listed below, and hope this practical advice will help you manage your business and the people you work with to achieve the desired results.

1. Managing Change
A brand needs to be regularly monitored, updated and/or changed as conditions in the marketplace indicate a change is needed.

Change should be carefully managed to maintain **consistency, continuity and memorability** of the brand's marketing communications. Be very careful about making sudden and drastic changes as it will confuse customers who have grown use to your current marketing messages. But when market conditions or consumer trends indicate a strategic change is needed, be prepared to invest the money to execute and establish the new or modified message for the brand or it will drop off the consumer radar for a period of time until the new changes eventually break through.

New client managers taking over the marketing communications program (from the previous manger) will often want to change things to make an impact and put their stamp on the marketing program for their own career motivations. Such actions cause disruptions and confusion internally and in the marketplace.

**Marketing programs tend to wear out much faster
inside the organization than they do with customers.**
Don't make changes for the sake of just doing something new and different; listen to the customer and the competitive environment and let them give you the signal that changes need to be made and why. Change is inevitable, necessary and vital, and needs to be managed skillfully.

The Intel Inside® and Dyson cases are outstanding examples of how to do this brilliantly.

2. Project Management

Things can go wrong very quickly if the communications and working process are not sorted out and agreed to at the outset. From my experience in the advertising agency business and as a consultant called in to solve problems, most of the time things go wrong because of this.

This is what needs to happen to make sure things run as smoothly and efficiently as possible understanding there will be intense moments of passion and healthy conflict along the way.

Communications
Identify all members in the marketing communications team (and other functions of the company that need to be involved), clarify roles, functions and responsibilities, determine who the decision-makers are and the chain of command, and establish how the team will communicate with each other and how often. Put it on paper and circulate it obtaining everyone's signature.

While e-mail, SMS, internal company networks, phone or video conferences can save time, by sharing work in progress, it can also build barriers. Allow for periodic meetings for everyone to meet face-to-face. Take the time to get to know each other and build tight relationships. If there is friction among any of the team members, this is the time to get it out in the open and resolve it. These meetings can take place in an office conference room, but ideally it is best to get out of the office for some unstructured time together over a meal or drinks, attending an event or engaging in a shared activity. It will make the project run much smoother, and a great team spirit and purpose will naturally evolve. Clients should do the same with their outside agency partners. This enhances the collaboration process and efficiency of virtual communications once a project is underway.

Working Process
Lay out an entire time-line for the project; identify all the tasks and deliverables. Clarify which outside agency partners are needed and have them build a parallel working process inside their organization to accomplish their part. Build in time for the approval process and revisions. Determine how to get all the work done on time, on budget and with the desired result. Publish this on paper and circulate, and again, ask everyone to sign it.

Project List

This document keeps track of all of the above. Agree on a format and amount of detail, assign one person to update it weekly and circulate it to the agreed distribution list. It keeps everyone on the same page, provides a road map on deliverables and acts as the *glue* to pull all aspects of the project together in one place. On an agreed regularly scheduled basis, pull all members of the marketing team and/or outside agency partners together (face-to-face or virtually) to review the project list: it is a valuable tool to measure progress and make sure nothing slips through the cracks. The project list is an effective way to keep management informed about what is going on and allows them to focus in on a particular item of interest.

Balancing of Time, Cost, Quality - TCQ

In planning the creative production of the marketing communications program, there are three vital elements to manage: time, cost and quality. You can only have two of these at a time.

If you want something produced quickly and to high-quality standards, there will be a production cost premium.

If you want something produced to high-quality standards with a limited budget, you need to allow more time to get it done.

If you want to produce something quickly with a limited budget, you will sacrifice quality.

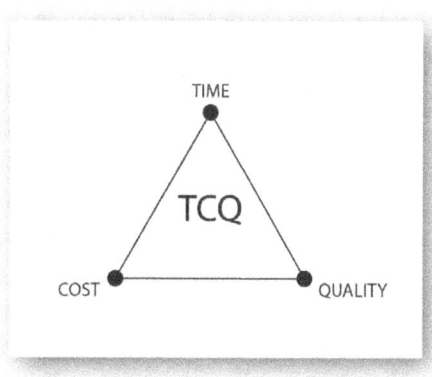

It is important to plan production schedules and budgets adequately so quality is never compromised.

This brings to mind something I've observed many times: **there is never enough time and budget to get it right at the outset, but there is always enough time and budget to redo it!**

For example, at the last minute, the head of marketing or the CEO unexpectedly checks up on the project in progress. He/She looks at everything and does not like it (reasons can be subjective or strategic). Or, maybe he/she was not part of the planning process or kept informed of the work-in-progress (via the project list), and suddenly he/she demands a different approach be taken. Everything is tossed in the trash. The client project team and outside agency partners are now in a panic to redo everything within an impossible deadline that will exceed the planned production budget. To avoid such a situation, go back to the start of this section and re-read!

Bottom line, business is about people collaborating. It is personal; your customers are people too. Always maintain a sense of humanity and humility, allowing for some human frailties. Numbers are just cold, hard facts; they do not live and breathe.

3. Silos and Politics

It is all too common in many companies that different functions become siloed or isolated from other functions by putting up walls (physical or virtual), developing a fortress mentality and protecting one's perceived sacred turf. There are many reasons why and how this happens; perhaps it is partly human nature. This is destructive to the business when vital information, wisdom and experience are not shared with internal alignment to achieve the goals or vision set by the CEO. It wastes massive amounts of time, money and unnecessary duplicated efforts, creates frustration and stress, and can cause people to seek another job elsewhere.

The same goes with politics; it is a fact of life. There are politics in everything we do, and they can get in the way. We learn to work with or around them to get things done. What should not be tolerated are *politicians* inside the organization who see their job as playing politics to enhance their own self-interest and trip up the working process. Politicians... Love them or leave them, belong in governmental elected offices, not in business.

The message that needs to be understood and respected by all stakeholders working on any project is *One Team, One Dream.* Act as a *bumble bee* moving from flower to flower pollinating and motivating fellow team members, exchanging information and sharing. Shoot the terrorists, and push out the troublemakers and non-team players.

4. Working With Outside Agencies

Building a productive working relationship
Please do not call the outside agencies vendors or suppliers. This sets up an adversarial *master and slave* attitude. Please accept them, and at all times, refer to them as outside agency partners. They have special skills the client organization does not possess. They should be welcomed into the CMO team and well-informed about the business, so that everyone is working collaboratively.

A company will require an advertising agency or any number of specialist marketing service suppliers (e.g., public relations, marketing research, media planning and buying, web/social/mobile/digital specialists, graphic designers, etc.) scaled to the size of the project to help plan, create and manage the brand marketing communications program. I collectively refer to them as *the agency.*

The agency's job is to provide the following:

- Voice of the consumer – key advisor on consumer and communication trends
- Outside point-of-view, bringing fresh *outside-the-box* thinking
- Business partnership
- Professionalism, experts in their area of specialization
- Clear recommendations and reasons why
- Knowledge of key business issues and what the competition is doing
- Motivation to go beyond what is expected and challenge the norm
- Contribute to all brand strategies
- Add value

Manage the agency based on the following:

- Pick them on their work, not reputation
- Make sure expectations are clear from the start
- Detailed plan for agency work, prepared in advance
- Be fair with time and money
- Give clear briefs with room for creativity
- Build multiple relationships with them
- Give honest, direct, regular feedback
- Don't blame them for work you have approved
- Help them to get inside your brand
- Don't expect them to own and run your brand

Everyone needs to be mindful of the pressure of deadlines and budgets. The client and agency need to work closely on planning the marketing calendar so that adequate time is allocated to developing and producing the communications program. Realistic budgets need to be established to accomplish all of the assigned tasks with the level of quality appropriate to the brand's promise. The agency needs to respect all agreed client deadlines, and the client has to approve the work when the agency requires them to do so. It is very often a high-pressure and emotionally charged working environment.

Please remember, agencies advise, the client has the ultimate responsibility to approve the work. The agency cannot produce anything or place it in any media without the client's official approval. Therefore, the client bears the final responsibility for marketing communications investments.

Trust and Respect

At all times, there needs to be a bond of *trust and respect* between all team members internally and with outside agency partners or the relationships will never be productive.

Importance of evaluation and fair compensation

A regular and structured agency evaluation process should be in place to judge their performance and fairly allow the agency to express grievances as to how it is directed and managed by the client; the relationship is a two-way street. There should be a formal review annually and with quarterly informal reviews if on a retainer contract, or at defined review points if on a short-term project-by-project basis. If the client is not happy with the agency's performance, then it needs to be addressed immediately, openly and frankly together, and worked on until a congenial consensus is reached. Personalities will often conflict and can change, but the relationship should endure. If the agency is not up to the job, the client should terminate the relationship and not drag things out, as it is destructive to both parties and the business.

Compensation needs to be fair and clear upfront. The agency is a business, and their business with the client must be profitable or it will **not** invest in the relationship. It will not put the best people on the brand, have the motivation to go above and beyond what is expected, and the brand will suffer the consequences with ineffective marketing communications and poor service. Both parties need to agree on the scope of work, terms of contract and compensation, and sign an agreement **before** any work begins.

Creativity

One of the most difficult areas to judge when working with an agency is the creative. A critical element in any communications program is to *break through* and be noticed by the intended target in the media. But creativity is not an end to itself; there is the danger of *creative masturbation.*

Client and agency have invested a lot of time and effort to develop a strategic brief to base the creative on and have decided which media it is to appear in. The client approves the brief before the agency starts the creative process. Now the agency returns to present the creative work.

First of all, does it address the key points in the brief? If not, the meeting should stop immediately and the agency should leave and return with work that does.

Judging the effectiveness of creative is a delicate balance of emotional and rational considerations. There is no guarantee that any creative idea is going to work: in a sense, every creative idea is a gamble. A lot of money must be invested to produce and run it in media.

It is very difficult to minimize personal opinion or reaction. Ninety percent of the time in every client creative presentation I have been in, the first thing the client says is, *"I like it"* or *"I don't like it,"* a personal, subjective reaction, and then the meeting starts to dangerously wander away from the agreed brief and into the realm of personal opinion.

Everyone has to put themselves into the mind of the prospect and look at the work from their realities, wants and needs. Does the creative work make sense? Does it meet the principles of K.I.S.S. and W.I.I.F.M.? The agency is pressing the client hard to buy something that they are passionate about, and the client should not be afraid to stand their ground on the creative, addressing the strategic business issues. This is a collaborative process.

Creativity must have a passion for supporting the brand promise and selling its points of differentiation. The agency may be harboring ambitions of winning a creative reward. Nice to have, but the only reward the client should be worried about is the vote of the customer, CEO and CFO to justify the creative output.

Creativity and effectiveness are not alternatives. Neither are they competitors, nor synonyms nor antonyms. In marketing communications, one is the means to the other.

Think of a joke and then think of laughter. It requires talent and originality to think of a joke and to tell it well. But a joke is not an end in itself: it is designed to achieve something called *laughter.*

You will only know for certain if your joke was a good one if and when people laugh. The longer (time) and the louder (decibel strength) they laugh, the better the joke. The joke (the thing) is measurable.

Evaluating creativity in a marketing program while ignoring its effectiveness is like holding an awards evening for jokes in the absence of an audience!

Finally, be aware of creative directors that have a favorite movie or song that they are looking for an unsuspecting client to build their advertising idea around to fulfill some creative fantasy. Good creative directors realize they are an extension of the selling process, not someone who failed to make it in the entertainment industry.

Importance of production values

When working with the agency on the creative process, please consider the importance of *production values*: the quality of the photography/filming, editing, music, casting, graphic design, copywriting, printing, programing and navigation that go into every piece of communication. If it looks cheap or is complicated and difficult to deal with, it reflects poorly on the brand and the impact will be negatively reflected in the KPIs. Make sure the look, tone and feel of the marketing communications lives up to the brand promise and experience. The production budget needs to be realistic without being wasteful. We are not supposed to judge a book by its cover, but all too often we do.

Know what they do

It is recommended the client visit the agency office, or at least meet the people working on the brand and be knowledgeable about what they do and how they do it. It will also help to understand, evaluate and approve all agency costs. The agency will also appreciate periodic client visits (but don't be a pest) and interest shown in what they are doing as partners on the same mission! It will help the clients directly interfacing with the agency to better direct them and support the work that has so much blood, sweat and tears invested in it.

To end this section, this is an example I often use with clients to explain the implications of all the above on agency costs and what they are eventually asked to pay.

Imagine you are in Tokyo staying at a hotel and need to buy a coat. The reason why you need to buy a coat is because the weather has suddenly turned cold and you did not bring one with you; so you set out to buy one. You are in a hurry, are not familiar with the mass transit system and decide to go by taxi. In this story, the taxi represents your outside agency.

When you get in the taxi and the door closes, you have signed a contract with the driver agreeing to the terms of service and stated menu of pricing (the meter). It is the driver's obligation to get you to your destination safely and courteously. The driver has GPS to get to your destination as quickly and directly as possible while avoiding traffic congestion and running up the meter.

You ask the driver to take you to Ginza, and as he starts driving the meter is activated. On the way to Ginza, you are tapping away on your smartphone looking for information on where to buy a coat. Upon arrival in Ginza, you decide that stores in Ginza may be too expensive. The meter reads ¥1,500, and you ask the driver to take you to Shibuya. You continue to tap away on the phone researching coats in Shibuya. Upon arrival you decide stores in Shibuya are too youthful. The meter now reads ¥5,000. You ask the driver to take you to Shinjuku as you continue to tap away on your phone.

Upon arrival in Shinjuku, you decide the stores there are too middle-of-the-market in terms of style options. Now the meter reads ¥8,000. You ask the driver to take you to Akihabara; you've decided to take a detour to look for an electronic gadget.

On the way to Akihabara, the weather is becoming noticeably worse. Upon arrival you decide the electronic gadget is not so important after all. The meter now reads ¥12,000. You decide to return to Ginza to buy the coat there. While the prices may be higher than other parts of the city, the greatest choice of coats is available there. The driver stops in front of the requested department store and asks you for ¥15,000, the amount on the meter. You are shocked at the price and say to the driver, *"Why is it so expensive? I just wanted to go to Ginza from my hotel!"* You have to pay the taxi driver the amount on the meter or you cannot get out.

How could this have been avoided? Doing your research before getting in the taxi so it would have been clear exactly where you wanted to go; consider this your strategic brief. You might have asked the driver (the agency) if he had any insights or suggestions on the best place to buy a coat based on his knowledge and network of contacts. Once underway, you forgot the reason for, or the purpose of, your journey and got side-tracked; poor process or project management. You ended up spending a lot more money on the taxi (agency fees) and now have less money to spend on the coat (production and media)!

PART 5

Marketing Communications Strategic Foundation Check List

It is time to do the hard work for **your** brand working in partnership with your outside agency partners and cross-functionally inside the company. This check list synthesizes all the analytical work to bring your brand communications strategic foundation into sharp focus. Work through this check list, complete what is most relevant, adapt and modify as needed.

√ Background

- If this is for a new product launch, what was the development process to arrive at the final product?
- If this is from an existing brand, summarize its history up to the present.

√ Use SWOT to focus on business issues marketing is to address, or business problem(s) to solve

- Summation of all competitive information and market research data
- Sales and market share performance/trends
- Consumer trends affecting segment or niche

√ Why does your brand (or company) exist?

√ What does it do?

√ How does it do it?

√ Who are your prospects?

- Describe their realities, wants and needs and motivations
- Describe them as people not statistics
- Add relevant demographic data

√ What is your brand promise?

√ Describe your brand experience at all customer contact points

√ Define the brand's points of differentiation

√ Position your brand in the mind of the prospect

√ Determine the single-minded message or USP

√ Tell your brand story

- Persuasion and reasons to believe
- K.I.S.S. and W.I.I.F.M.

√ Determine which media your prospects are interacting with and influenced by

- Develop a media plan and task budget (what you can justify asking for but will not likely get, so set the media list in descending priority)
- Communications logistics between one-way and two-way media
- Consider experiential events and sponsorships

√ Marketing communications deliverables – list in detail

- What you plan to produce (e.g., advertising, brochures, website, etc.)
- What you plan to run (e.g., events, trade shows, exhibitions, sponsorships, etc.)

√ PR plan to engage the press

- Press engagement events (e.g., press conferences, company visits, executive interviews, etc.)
- Press information package

√ Investigate needs of the sales team

- Presentation material to gain distribution
- Marketing communications or promotional actions to pull or push sales through pipeline
- Training material and support for sales associates

√ Marketing investment measurement criteria

- Objectives
- Outcome scenarios – best case to worst case and contingency planning
- KPIs
- ROI metrics

√ Select outside agency partners and establish working agreements

- Established agency partners - brief
- Need for new or additional outside resources – identify, select and brief
- Agency evaluation process and criteria
- Agency compensation and terms of business

√ Define the mandatories that need to be reflected in all communications

- Brand identity framework, slogan, logo, legal requirements, etc.
- Continuity and consistency with previous communications, assess need for change

√ Budget – Funding marketing program

- Internal resources and outside agency compensation
- Production of communications deliverables/assets
- Media and PR

√ Establish and publish project timeline and working process

- Internal and with outside agencies
- Seamlessly speak to the customer with one voice and break down internal silos so everyone is singing from the same sheet of brand music

Add other areas relative to your business.

Bob-san's Life Journey

Personal & Professional Summary

I am an American of Swedish and English ancestry. I was born in Rochester, New York in 1953. My father is from Belleville, New Jersey, and my mother from New Canaan, Connecticut (both in the New York City metro area). My father was an executive with General Electric (GE); his career spanned nearly 40 years in finance, accounting and international operations. My mother always kept a beautiful home, made all holidays, birthdays and family vacations special, and was a great asset to my father's career. I have one younger brother who is an attorney.

I grew up in the glory days of America in the 1950s and 60s. We owned American cars and we ate only American food. We considered ourselves upper-middle class. We always lived in a suburban private house. I attended public schools. I spent my childhood (ages 2-10) in Fairfield, Connecticut within the TV influence of New York City. I played outside with other children in the neighborhood, and we went everywhere on our bicycles (without helmets). We did not have structured sports programs and our parents did not supervise what we did as long as we came home on time for dinner. We used our imaginations and made our own fun.

From when I was 10, my father began to move us around as his GE career progressed, and thus began a lifetime of moving. We moved to Allentown, Pennsylvania; back to Fairfield, Connecticut; to Cleveland,

Ohio (where I went to high school); and in 1970, my father took an assignment in Manila, Philippines. During the time we were there, we traveled to Hong Kong and Taiwan, and my first trip to Japan was in June 1971. This was my first taste of the *expat life*, and I loved it.

From Manila, I went back to the USA to attend Marietta College in Marietta, Ohio, starting in August 1972. My father was transferred to Mexico City in 1973. I traveled around Mexico during my college years with my parents and brother.

I studied theater arts, mass communications and marketing, and held a number of leadership positions in campus organizations. I am a member of the Delta Tau Delta fraternity and served as chapter president.

Upon graduation in 1976, I joined Procter & Gamble's (P&G) paper products division (Pampers, Bounty and Charmin brands) as a sales representative in New York City – a tough place to learn to sell. In two years I learned all I could from P&G's intensive training, moved to the advertising industry in September 1978, and followed my passion to become an *ad man* on Madison Avenue. I started with Ted Bates Advertising (the USP agency) working on Colgate toothpaste. Then, as young account executives frequently do to bump their salary, I moved to SSC&B Lintas where I worked on the Lysol Spray account, and in September 1981, I made the move to Dancer Fitzgerald Sample (DFS), initially working on the launch of 3M's *Post-it Notes®*. DFS also handled all of the advertising for Toyota in the USA and Canada.

In January 1982, I was invited to take on a new international assignment in Japan. DFS was starting a new project with Toyota's global headquarters in Tokyo... Was I interested in going over? It was an easy answer. In February 1982, I began my new life in Japan as a 29 year old bachelor. What started out as a two-year assignment evolved into a lifetime relationship with Japan.

I didn't speak a word of Japanese, knew nothing of Japanese business practices and had no experience working with Toyota or the car business.

But I had been well trained in the fundamentals of sales, marketing and advertising.

Our mission was to build a global relationship with Toyota and transfer our success with Toyota USA's advertising to Toyota's global marketing and advertising programs. We faced a formidable task. Eventually, we earned our way into Toyota's global business and were awarded with more and more assignments as our Tokyo Toyota team grew.

Those were some of the most challenging and difficult years of my life and career, adapting to living in Japan and the inner workings of Toyota. But I had a vision of what the long-term potential could be and did whatever it took to endure and build a career around Toyota inside the agency.

I met my wife, Yumi, in August 1983 at a film studio shooting a TV commercial for Toyota. She was born and grew up in Tokyo. Yumi worked for an ad agency in Tokyo after graduating from Seijo University, and eventually went to New York City to study English for one year and then spent three years in Santa Monica, California studying professional make-up in Hollywood. She earned a series of professional certifications and retuned to Tokyo and became a freelance make-up artist for the film and advertising production industry. Her father, Hideo Kadoi, is the founder of Hitachi Maxell (audio/videotape and batteries), which he built into a successful global brand. He was presented two special awards by the Showa Emperor for his various business activities. He was a great inspiration and mentor to me.

I married Yumi in December 1984. Our first son, Robert, was born in October 1985, and second son, Andrew, in June 1987, both in Tokyo. Yumi stopped working to raise the children and help support my career.

DFS was purchased by Saatchi & Saatchi in 1986; through Saatchi we had a much bigger and stronger global network to expand and increase our services to Toyota.

In September 1988, I was transferred to Saatchi's Los Angeles, California office to gain experience on the Toyota USA account as a strategic planner; plus, it was at the time we formed the Team One agency to launch the new Lexus brand.

In March 1990, I was transferred back to Japan to take responsibility for our global Toyota HQ relationship and acted as the global coordinator of all Saatchi's Toyota and Lexus activities outside the USA – we had grown to over 30 distributor relationships around the world.

In 1994, I was asked to move to Brussels, Belgium to help support (from the agency side) the start-up of Toyota Europe's new headquarters. Over the next few years, I built up the business between Saatchi and Toyota Europe.

In 1998, I reached a turning point in my life and was feeling the time had come to move on. I look back on my years with Saatchi with great satisfaction and pride; the connections and experience gained have resonated ever since.

I officially left Saatchi at the end of February 1999 as a resident of Belgium. I took a cold hard look at my collective knowledge and career experience. I decided to continue an expat lifestyle and remain outside the USA. But I had to learn to survive on my own.

I realized that I am happiest in my work and life when engaged in entrepreneurial activity. I am energized and motivated starting new projects, initiating new assignments proactively, and taking on tough, complicated situations and sorting them out. I have a very high threshold for risk. Whatever my official job description, I always exceeded it and redefined it. I developed a reputation for making things happen and getting things done while gaining the trust and respect of my clients and agency colleagues.

I decided to start my own one-man virtual consultancy and named it after *Lake Wickaboag* in West Brookfield, Massachusetts where my family has had a summer home since 1908.

I wanted the flexibility and freedom to work anywhere at any time and with whomever I wanted to get the job done, and positioned myself as a *Problem Solver*.

I also decided that I did not want to end my relationship with Toyota and needed to find a different way to continue our working relationship while also developing many new business skills and additional clients. So I had to reinvent myself and expand my horizons beyond the advertising agency business.

I then began the process of working through my network of contacts, and relatively quickly a number of companies asked me to step into their businesses. I also went to Japan to see the people at the Toyota headquarters I felt closest to so they would know what had happened to me, why and what I was hoping to do, and seek their advice and counsel.

To make things even more interesting, my wife and I decided to live in Italy and we bought a home in the countryside outside of Rome. I ran my professional activities from an office in the house. In the summer months I worked from my Lake Wickaboag family home. I made frequent business trips to Japan across the year. I was living in Italy, Japan and the USA at various times throughout the year, and running my business from wherever I happened to be thanks to laptops, e-mail, mobile phones and airplanes.

I won retained consulting assignments from Japanese, American and European clients.

I developed the ability to work on a wide variety of projects simultaneously in different parts of the world while managing my business affairs with no staff. I connect into each of my client's organizations and work with their people and resources. I have a network of contacts in specialized areas I can tap into on an as needed basis. Low overhead and maximum flexibility enable me to deliver what is needed with the desired result.

In early 2008, I sensed the coming economic problems facing Europe, so Yumi and I decided to sell our property in Rome and return to Japan. I also felt it was the right time to move my consulting practice to Tokyo and focus on Japan and the USA. We relocated to Tokyo in January 2009. We split our time between Tokyo and my family home on Lake Wickaboag. Our two sons live in the New England area.

In 2014, Yumi established her own company in Japan, MIMIKO, INC., and expanded it to the USA in 2015. She designed and developed facial wrinkle flattening patches. They are sold in Japan via SHO-BI under the MAGiE Lab brand. In the USA they are sold under the brand name *Toute Nuit* (French meaning *every night*). I am her marketing consultant, and so far the business is exceeding expectations, with further ambitions to expand globally. www.toutenuit.com

My name Robert Eric Peterson is a mouthful to pronounce in the Japanese language; *Peterson-san* is particularly cumbersome, plus there are too many *Rs*; a hard letter to pronounce in Japanese. I go by the nickname Bob anyway, so the Japanese call me **Bob-san**; easy to remember and pronounce. It has become my professional brand identity around the world.

Requests, Initiatives, Curiosity over 10 Years That Formed This Book - Story in Three Parts

The **first part** of the story started in April 2003 during a business trip to Tokyo. At the end of a meeting with Yoshio Ishizaka, at the time Executive Vice-President of Toyota Motor Corporation and responsible for all operations outside Japan including marketing, he completely caught me by surprise with a request to make a presentation as a guest speaker for Toyota's internal veterans lecture series. This was a heavily promoted internal event held once or twice a year, at which a prominent Toyota sales and marketing executive would make a presentation about his experience to members of the various departments related to Toyota's global operations in the Tokyo and Toyota City offices. This was designed to share wisdom and experience, and motivate younger staff. I was the first person outside the company invited to speak, so I asked Ishizaka-san, *"Why me?"* He felt I had a unique global perspective on their business, and having worked on their marketing and advertising for over 20 years, he thought I might have something interesting to say. He also thought my lifestyle and way of working were unique and an interesting side story too.

Of course I said yes and then asked him, *"What do you want me to talk about?"* He said, *"Anything you want!"* That was both a blessing and a curse, as I immediately felt the heaviness of the obligation. We set the date for the presentation to be in November. I spent the next few months thinking about what I wanted to say and present in the two-hour time slot. What I concluded was that Toyota needed a "back to basics" lecture about marketing and advertising, as I felt my greatest barrier to overcome working with my Toyota clients over the years was their lack of basic training in marketing. In September, I wrote to Ishizaka-san about the purpose and intent of my presentation with an outline. It received an immediate approval with no comments. This added to the heaviness of the obligation.

Putting this presentation together forced me to go back and think about everything I had learned through on-the-job experiences; and from my various mentors and agency training programs over the years. I also researched some relevant books and articles, and then went to work. The final presentation contained 132 slides and a number of videos of Toyota and Lexus TV commercials plus other examples. It was titled: *Making Things Happen A 20-Year Perspective on Toyota's Global Marketing & Advertising.* I boldly ended the presentation with eight *right-between-the-eyes* recommendations on what Toyota needed to do organizationally to improve how it manages and creates its marketing communications. I put on an informative and entertaining 90-minute presentation and left time for Q&A.

I presented to 400+ executives, managers and staff in Tokyo and Toyota City and received thunderous applause. Some of the attendees immediately did do some of the things I recommended, but fundamentally nothing really changed inside Toyota. Ishizaka-san had hoped my presentation would be the catalyst of change. But what we all learned is that one presentation alone cannot change anything unless it is backed by a follow-up program with management support and pressure to push it into the organization until it has the desired impact on daily operations.

Some of the content from that presentation has found its way into this book, and I thank Ishizaka-san for the great honor to make the presentation and forcing me to go back and think about everything I ever learned in order to share it. We remain close friends and see each other frequently.

The **second part** of the story is tied to Marietta College, where I earned my Bachelor of Arts degree in 1976. In the spring of 2005, I was visiting the campus and discovered the McDonough Leadership Center was starting a new Executive-in-Residence (EIR) program. They asked me if I would be the second EIR for the 2006/2007 academic year, focusing on my area of expertise; marketing and communications. Of course, I accepted and was given an open brief to do what I wanted. Another heavy obligation!

What I learned from my Toyota lecture experience is that a series of lectures is not effective if you really want someone to learn and put the information to practical use. Within hours or days of a lecture, the impact or message fades away as you go back to the daily tasks in front of you.

In January 2006, I submitted a proposal to create a *Communications Challenge* between competing teams of students to plan and execute a communication program for an existing business in the Marietta area – direct hands-on, real world experience. The proposal was accepted and implemented.

This started six months of preparation working closely with the college to select the teams of students, local businesses (the clients), and plan out the program and lectures. The program kicked off in August with a campus visit to meet students, their clients and to deliver a series of lectures on client management, communication planning, creative process and a list of project deliverables. I left the campus and returned to my normal business activities. I followed the students' progress by e-mail, project blogs and conference calls to guide them.

I returned to the campus the last two weeks of October to coach the teams through to their final presentations to a faculty panel, and ultimately their clients. The students went from zero to a full client presentation in eight weeks, their business analysis, communication plan, strategic brief, ideas and creative recommendations to their respective clients was at a professional level. Their clients were surprised and impressed by the student's ideas and recommendations.

In addition to overseeing the *Communications Challenge*, I lectured in advertising, PR, integrated communications, leadership, marketing, and international business management classes as well as advised students interested in an international business career or the communications field.

As a follow-up, I helped the college redesign its curriculum for the communications and mass media department. The *Communications Challenge* has been established as an ongoing cross-functional program for marketing and communications studies. I continue to advise this program and visit the campus when I can to consult with the professors and coach students. All the learning from this experience has gone into this book.

The **third part** of the story started in February 2010 in Tokyo. The impact of the Lehman shock and downturn of the global economy in 2009 hit the global car industry very hard, and Toyota was no exception. In early 2010, Toyota experienced the full impact of its *quality crisis* in the USA due to the potential danger of an accelerator being stuck against a floor mat and accusations of unintended acceleration incidents. It turned into a media circus and Akio Toyoda, Toyota Motor Corporation CEO, was called before the US Congress and grilled. This crisis spread globally and the potential damage to Toyota's brand reputation for quality, reliable, dependable vehicles was at severe risk. Combined with the global economic meltdown, this was a double-whammy for Toyota and an unprecedented challenge for any company to deal with.

As a *friend-of-Toyota* and deeply concerned about what was a happening, I spent a weekend in February 2010 proactively writing an analysis of what was taking place, risk to the brand, an assessment of Toyota's internal marketing and communications organization and its difficulty dealing with the situation, and made a recommendation for a program to address this.

This was presented to executives of Toyota Motor Corporation (TMC) and Toyota Motor Sales & Marketing Corporation (TMSM) in March 2010 as my proactive recommendations to respond to the global quality crisis, new competitive challenges, rapid changes in consumer behavior and media consumption.

The proposed program was *green lighted* in April 2010, and I was given the assignment to organize and *make it happen* with TMSM as the sponsor. The program's focus was on global brand management and marketing organizational/operational best practices and aligning them with Akio Toyoda's corporate vision. We also identified the critical issues facing the brand short-term. We also wanted to learn from some of the world's leading marketers by bringing in outside experts.

Based on my recommendation and with Toyota's permission, I recruited and teamed-up with Jim Stengel to develop and deliver the program. Working off of my brief, we developed the **Toyota Brand Forum (TBF)** in tight partnership with the TMSM clients between July and December 2010. Toyota's marketing executives from USA, Japan, China, Australia, Asia, Saudi Arabia, Europe and Brazil were invited to be the core participates – this group represents 70% of Toyota's global sales. Plus, observers joined from TMC, TMSM, Toyota regional sales and marketing organizations, and Toyota's *Global Knowledge Center*.

The first TBF meeting was held at UCLA's Anderson School of Management on January 27-29, 2011. The program included presentations from

Google, Facebook and a case study from Antonio Lucio – VISA Global Marketing Officer. Plus, we gave an assignment to a select group of MBA students to work on and present to the group. We also conducted hands-on workshops related to reforming Toyota's brand platform. It was a 3-day marketing MBA crash course led by Jim, with case studies from P&G and other brands. We held a follow-up meeting at Toyota's Nagoya office on June 8-10, 2011. We concluded the TBF with a presentation to senior executives in the TMC boardroom. I prepared the final reports and recommended actions from these meetings and distributed them to all attendees and TMC management via TMSM. The program was turned over to TMC and TMSM to manage and carry on internally.

Everything I learned from this experience is in this book. It was a privilege and thrill to work with Jim, and I appreciate everything he shared and taught me. Plus, he opened doors into other organizations I would never have had contact with otherwise.

Can I Help You?

My sales representative training at Procter & Gamble taught me to *ask for the order*!

If what I have written in this book makes sense and you would like to apply it to your business, please contact me in English or Japanese:

bobsanmakeithappen@gmail.com

But there are three conditions:

1) The CEO, business owner or leadership team must be directly involved
2) There must be flexibility to make organizational changes that elevate the role of marketing to a core function of the business
3) There must be practical application through a hands-on pilot project

In closing, I would like to leave you with one of my favorite quotes:

"I love it when a plan comes together!" - Colonel John "Hannibal" Smith, from The A-Team TV series.

Thank you for reading this book!

Bob-san speaking at the 12th CLSA Japan Forum February 27, 2015. This forum is Japan's most comprehensive annual event for global financial analysts. www.clsa.com

Acknowledgements

This book is the summation of everything I have learned to date in my professional career. I was able to make this book happen thanks to the time and interest of the following people, who devoted themselves to reading numerous drafts and providing their frank comments and suggestions.

Hirotaka Takeuchi – Professor of Management Practice @ Harvard Business School, previously Professor Graduate School of International Corporate Strategy @ Hitotsubashi University

Roberto De Vido – Editor

- Principal One Man Band Productions
- Co-founder at Empathy Digital
- Based in Kanagawa, Japan

Thomas Gerrard – Editor

- President, Communication Professionals Co., Ltd. in Tokyo, Japan
- President, Gerrard Global Initiatives in Los Angeles, California

Robert Kadoi Peterson – Oldest son, entrepreneurial professional with experience in brand and product development; and starting own company. Multi-lingual: English, Japanese, Italian, French & Spanish. Lives in Boston, Massachusetts www.linkedin.com/in/robertkpeterson

David Stokols – President, Automotive Marketing Consultants, Inc. (AMCI) in Los Angeles, California

Tom McGuire – President, NAVIS International in Brussels, Belgium

Koichi Hama – Design Consultant, Koichi Hama & Company in Tokyo, Japan

Tim Kennedy – Principal, Input Creative Group in Greenwich, Connecticut

Eric Wedemeyer – CEO, TACTUS Associates, Inc. in Tokyo, Japan

Honyaku Plus Translation Services in Tokyo, Japan

- Japanese adaptation of this book

About the Author

Robert Eric Peterson (REP) is President of the Wickaboag Consulting Group, Inc., a marketing and communications *problem-solving* consultancy that *makes things happen*. REP is highly regarded for his energy, enthusiasm, curiosity, tenacity, sense of humor, entrepreneurial spirit, willingness to take risks and ability to *get things done*. A global client management and strategic planning executive, consultant and change-*agent* for over 38 years, his work has spanned fast-moving consumer goods to the automotive industry and general business with an extensive network of contacts. His specialty is starting new projects and building new operations – or – taking on difficult situations, fixing them and turning them around. He has the ability to adapt quickly and easily to new working environments and cultures. He began his business career with Proctor & Gamble, moved to the advertising agency business in NYC, eventually spending 18 years at DFS/Saatchi & Saatchi before setting up his own consulting practice in 1999. He has lived and worked in NYC, Los Angeles, Tokyo, Brussels and Rome, and has traveled to 40+ countries on business projects during his career. He is constantly on the move. He has inspired the many multinational teams and students he has worked with. He has unique knowledge of the Japanese market and experience working with Japanese clients, becoming widely known as **Bob-san**. He has worked with Toyota Motor Corporation HQ in Japan, its Toyota and Lexus regional offices and distributors around the world since 1982, and a wide range of clients over the years in Japan, USA and Europe. He is a graduate of Marietta College; in 2006, he was invited by the McDonough Leadership Center to be an Executive-in-Residence. In 2013, he started lecturing and publishing articles about Japanese companies and marketing. REP is married with two sons, and splits his time between residences in Ota-ku, Tokyo, Japan and Lake Wickaboag, West Brookfield, Massachusetts, USA.

https://www.linkedin.com/in/repetersonbobsan

References

Rick Weitzman – Executive Director, Drucker Institute – e-mail and phone consultation confirming Peter Drucker's quotes and their proper usage

http://www.druckerinstitute.com/

Competitive Strategy Techniques for Analyzing Industries and Competitors
Michael E. Porter

Can Japan Compete?
Michael E. Porter, Hirotaka Takeuchi and Mariko Sakakibara

Advertising Age: www.adage.com/bigdataguide2014

Start With WHY? How Great Leaders Inspire Everyone to Take Action
Simon Sinek

TED TALKS: http://www.ted.com/talks/simon_sinek_how_great_leaders_inspire_action.html

Aaker on Branding 20 Principles That Drive Success
David Aaker

Brand Simple How Brands Keep It Simple and Succeed
Allen P. Adamson

Books by Jack Trout:

- *Differentiate or Die!* Survival in Our Era of Killer Competition
- *Trout on Strategy* Capturing Mindshare Conquering Markets
- *Big Brands Big Trouble* Lessons Learned the Hard Way
- *The Power of Simplicity* A Management Guide to Cutting Through The Non sense And Doing Things Right
- *In Search of the Obvious* The Antidote for Today's Marketing Mess
- Plus numerous articles in *Advertising Age*

Positioning: The Battle for Your Mind
Al Reis and Jack Trout

The Tipping Point
Malcolm Gladwell

All Marketers Tell Stories Why Authenticity Is the Best Marketing of All
Seth Godin

Buyology Truth and Lies About Why We Buy
Martin Lindstrom

GROW How Ideals Power Growth and Profit at the World's Greatest Companies
Jim Stengel

Where Good Ideas Come From The Natural History of Innovation
Steven Johnson

PRODUCT MANAGAMENT Fourth Edition
Donald R. Lehman and Russell S. Winner
Part of McGraw-Hill/Irwin Series in Marketing

Intel Ingredient Branding Case Study 2005
Intangible Business, Joint Managing Director Stuart Whitwell

InterBrand 2014 Best Global Brands http://www.bestglobalbrands.com/2014/ranking/

Intel and Dyson websites

Collection of articles from Jeremy Bullmore's weekly column, *Ask Jeremy. On the Campaign Couch*.
Published in the United Kingdom by *Campaign* which is dedicated to celebrating creative excellence in the communications industry whilst putting creativity firmly in a business context. Part of Brand Republic Group's sister Haymarket publication brands.

Appendix

Robert E. Peterson articles in 2012, 2013 and 2014

ADVERTISING AGE
http://adage.com/article/guest-columnists/japan-s-ultimate-challenge-marketing/242775/

BTRAX
Part 1
English: http://blog.btrax.com/en/2013/12/12/why-japanese-companies-struggle-with-marketing/
Japanese: http://blog.btrax.com/jp/2014/01/26/japanese-companies-marketing/
Part 2
English: http://blog.btrax.com/en/2014/03/17/how-japan-can-embrace-marketing/
Japanese: http://blog.btrax.com/jp/2014/04/07/japanese-companies-marketing-2/

WALL STREET JOURNAL QUOTE
http://online.wsj.com/article/SB100014240527023038129045772953120
31215188.html?mod=WSJ_auto_IndustryCollection

www.ingramcontent.com/pod-product-compliance
Lightning Source LLC
Chambersburg PA
CBHW070816180526
45168CB00002B/638